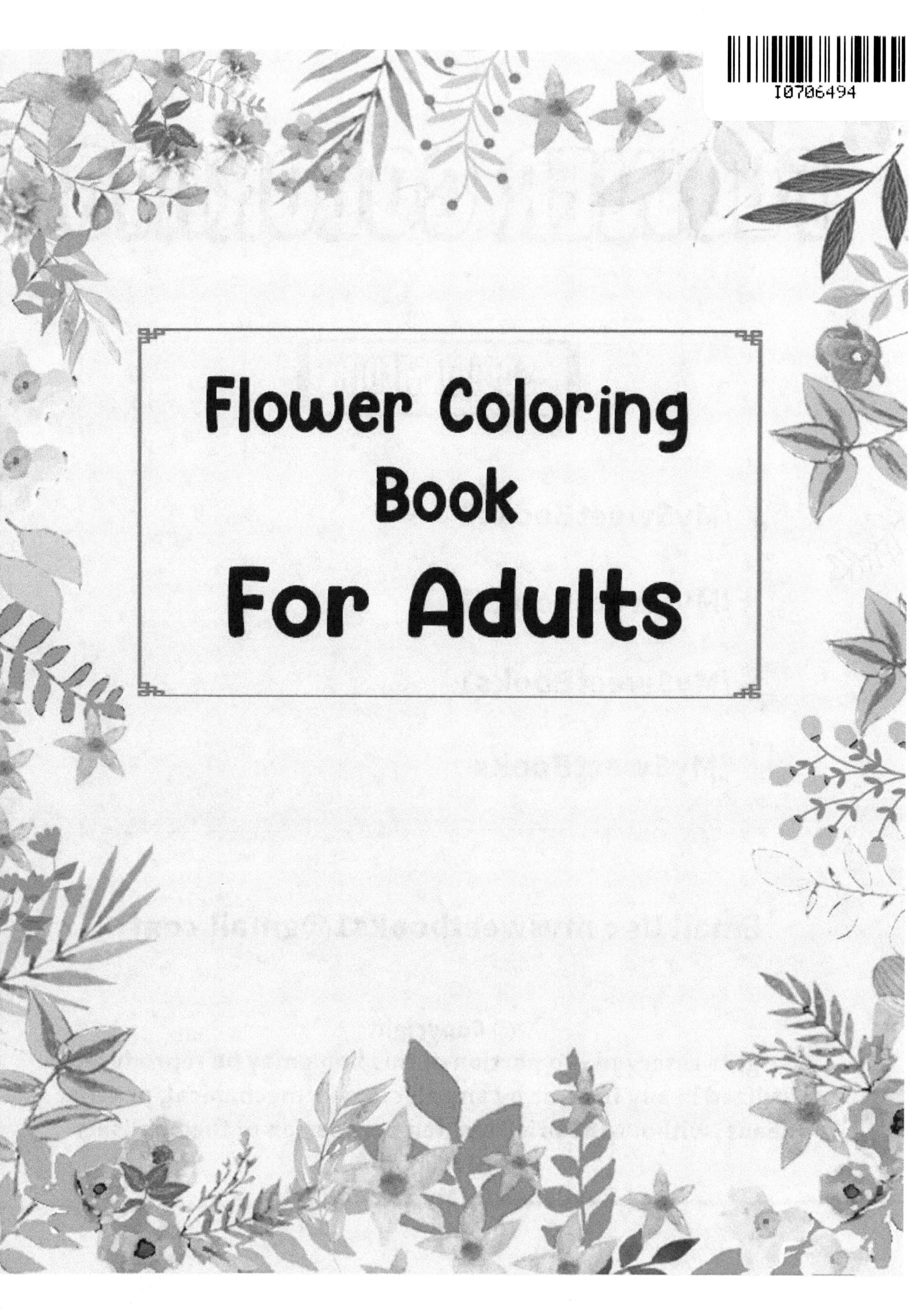

Flower Coloring
Book
For Adults

FLOWER COLORING

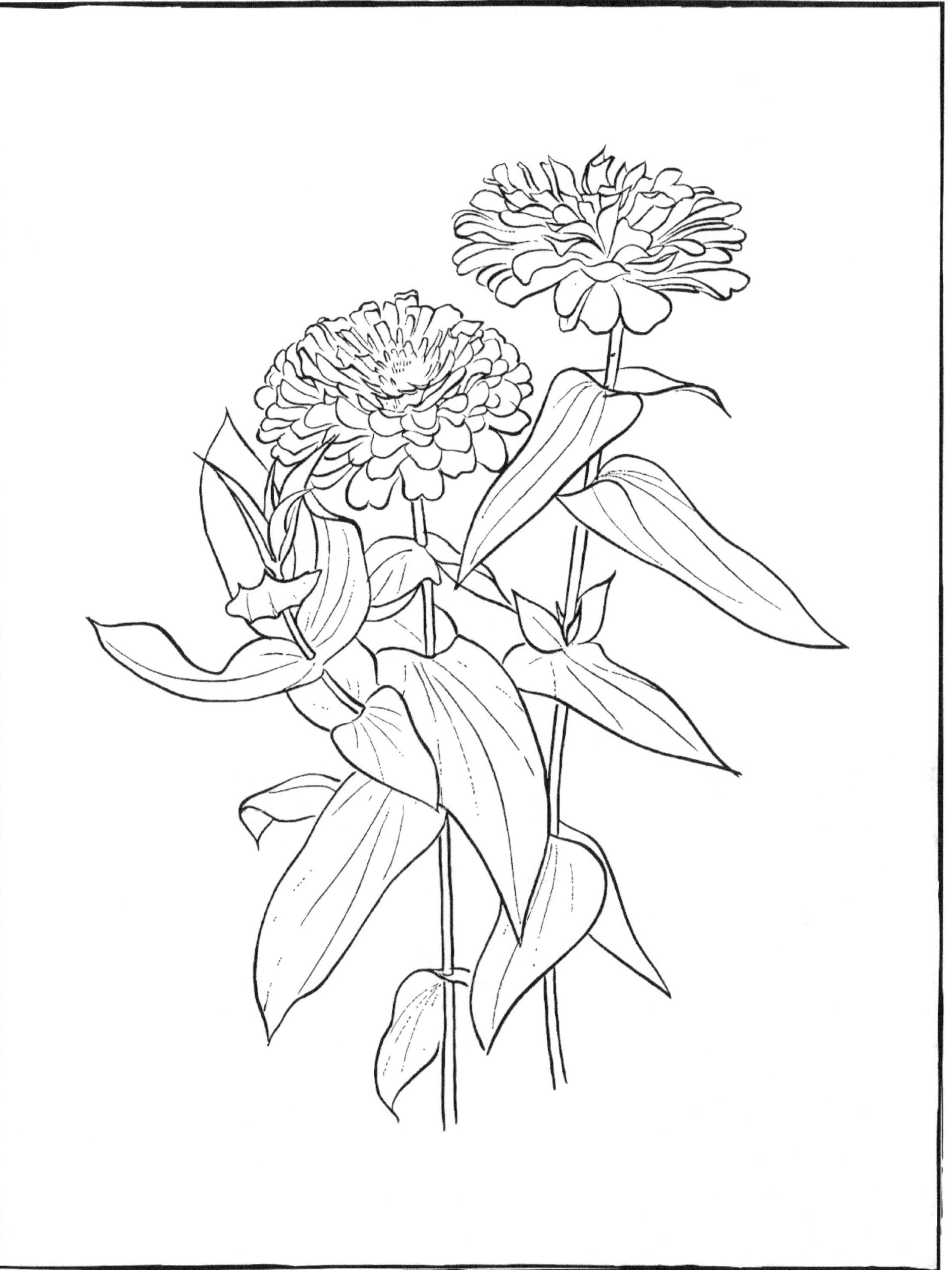

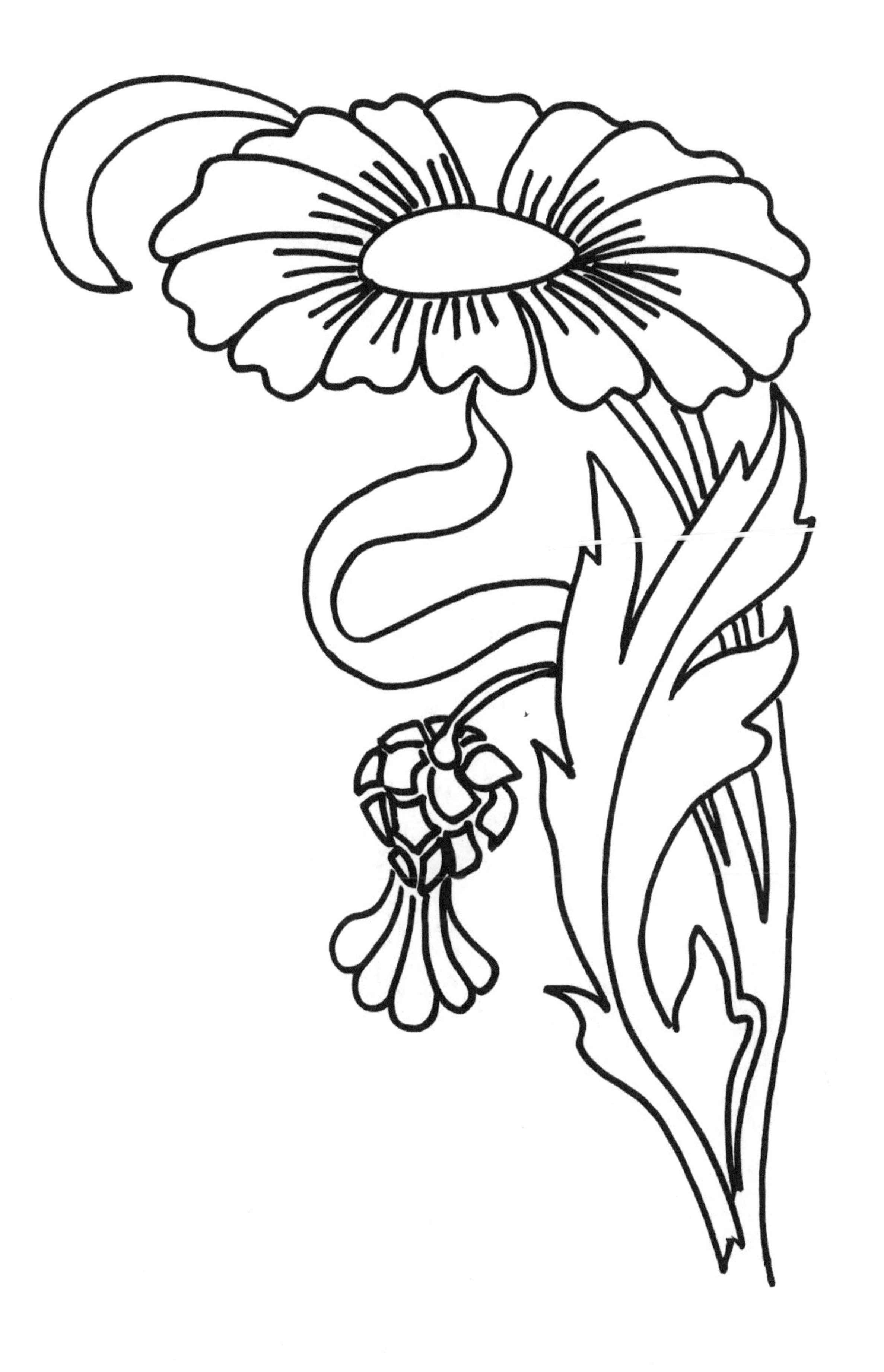

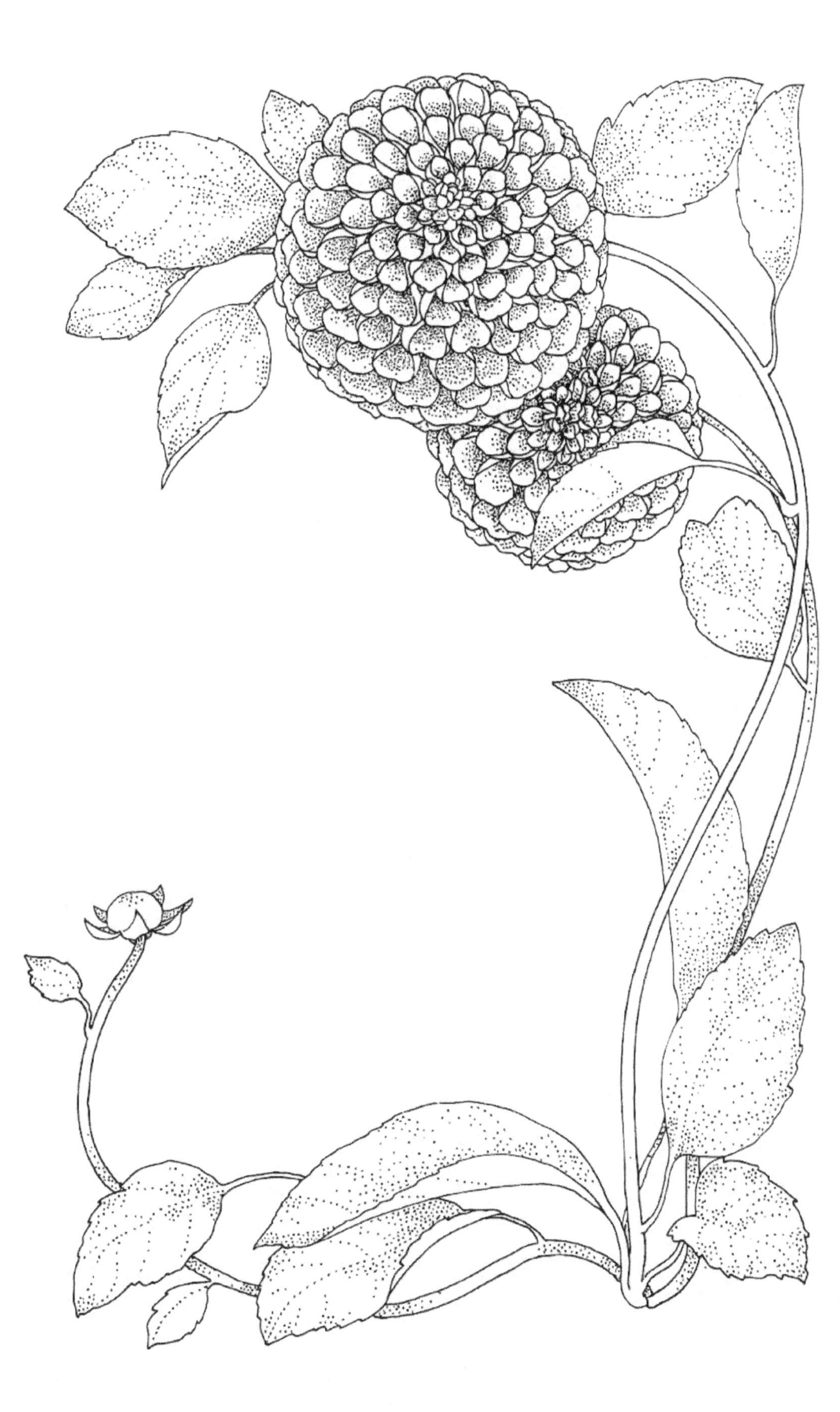

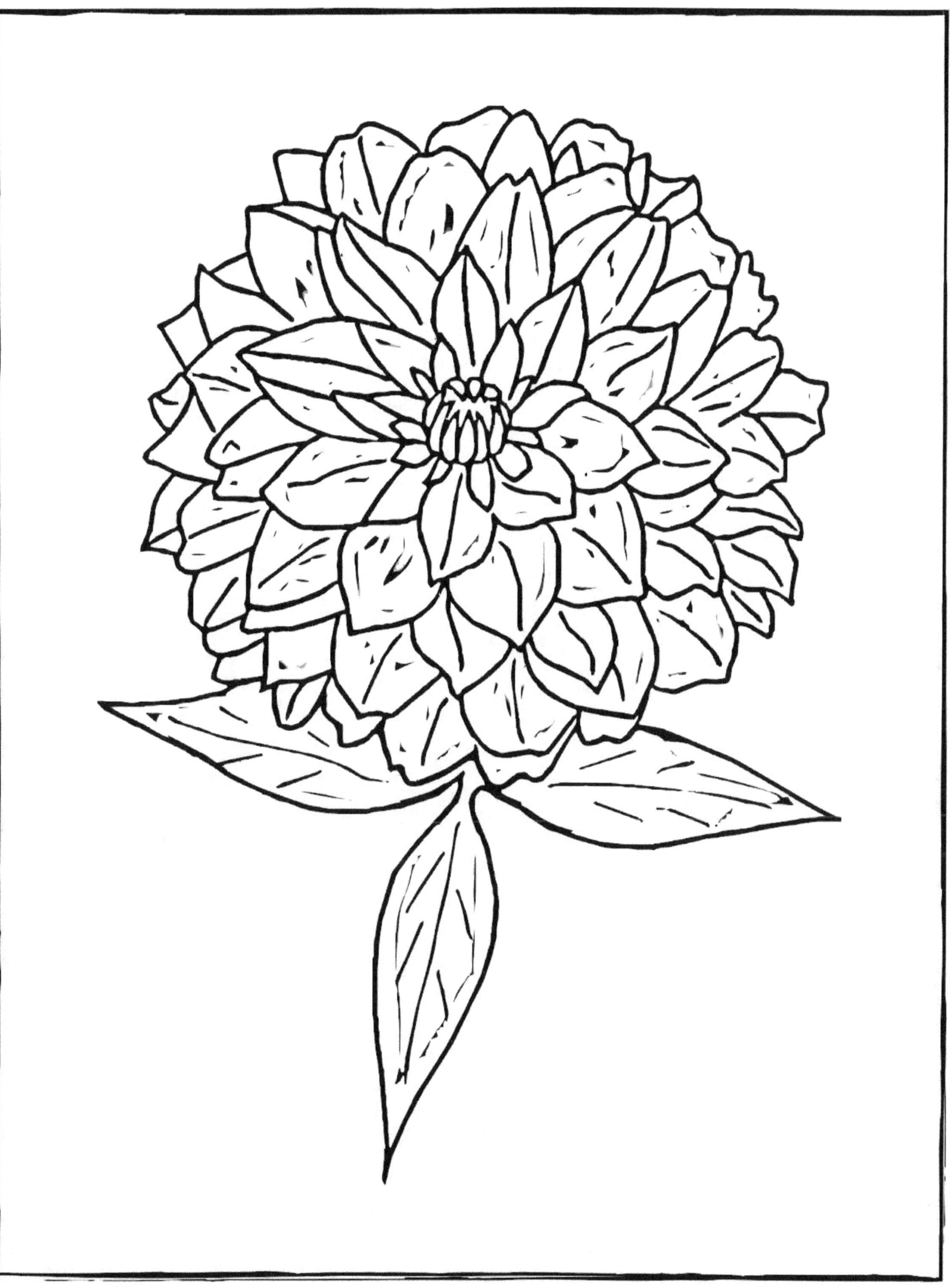

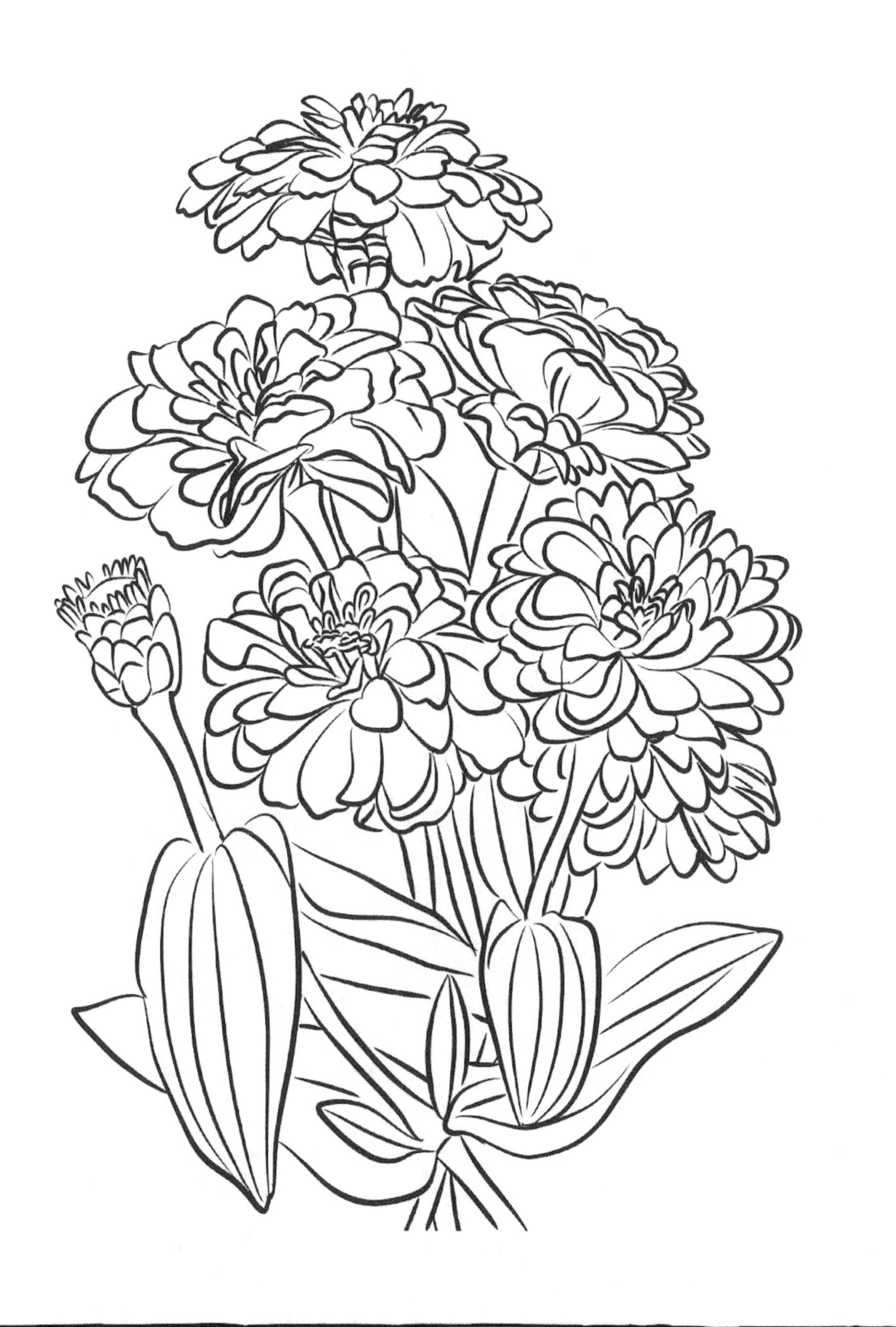

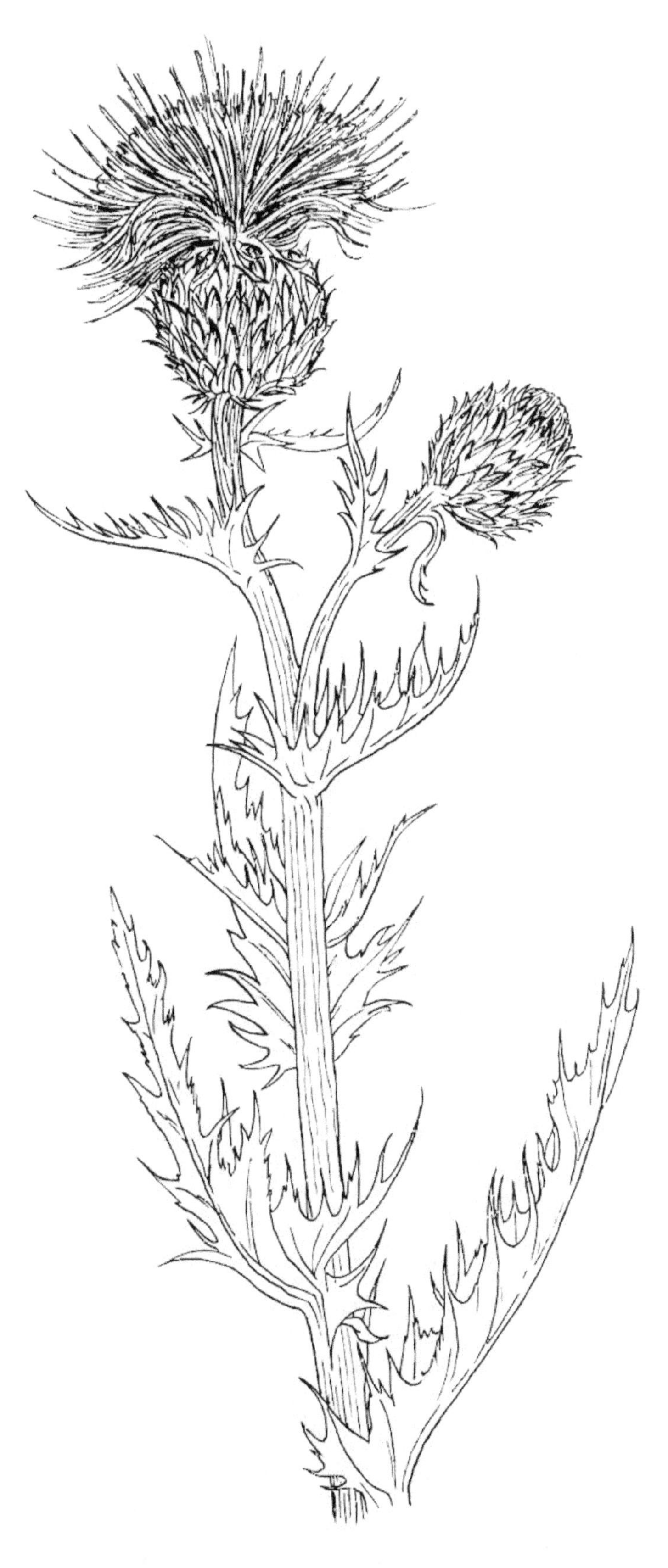

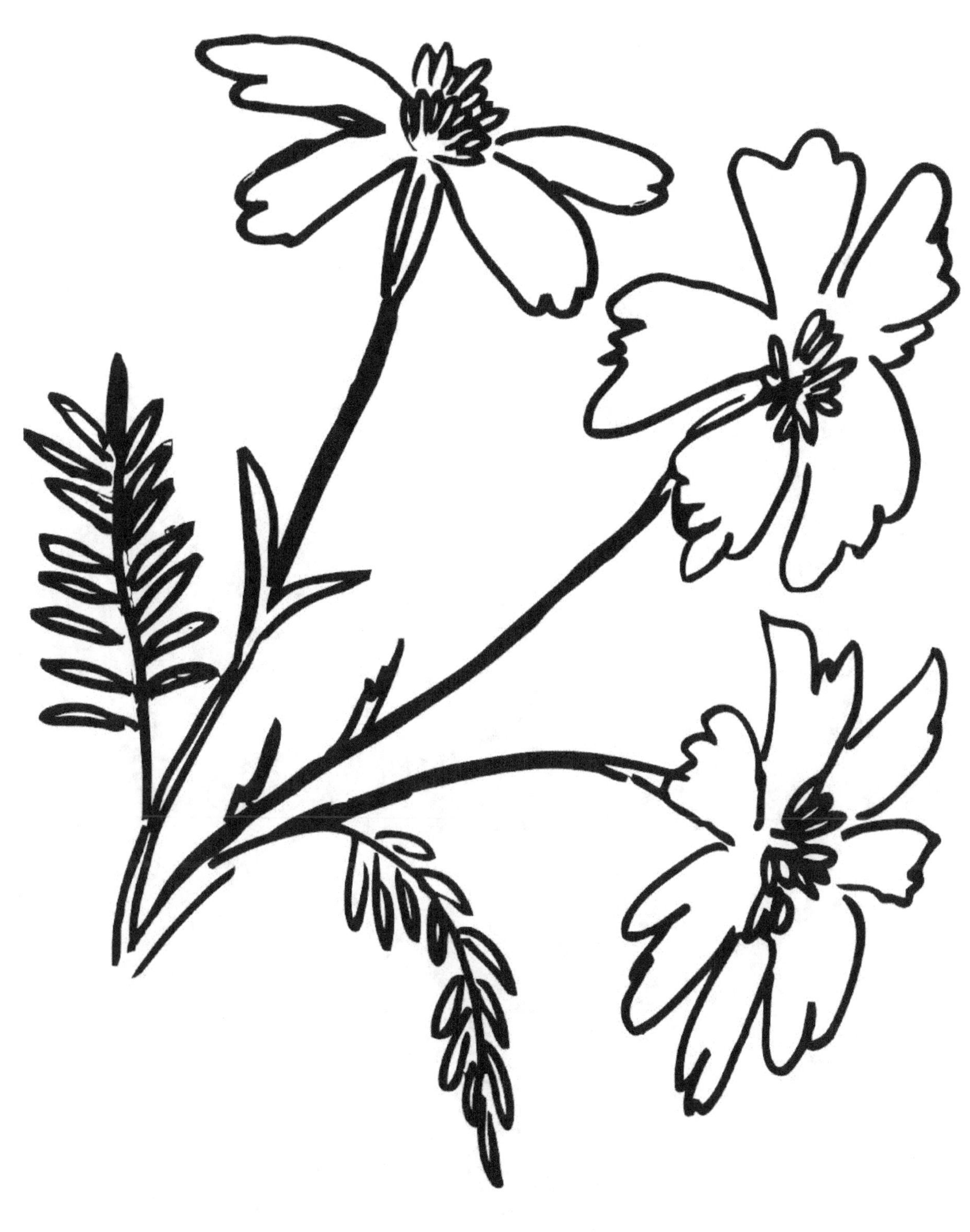

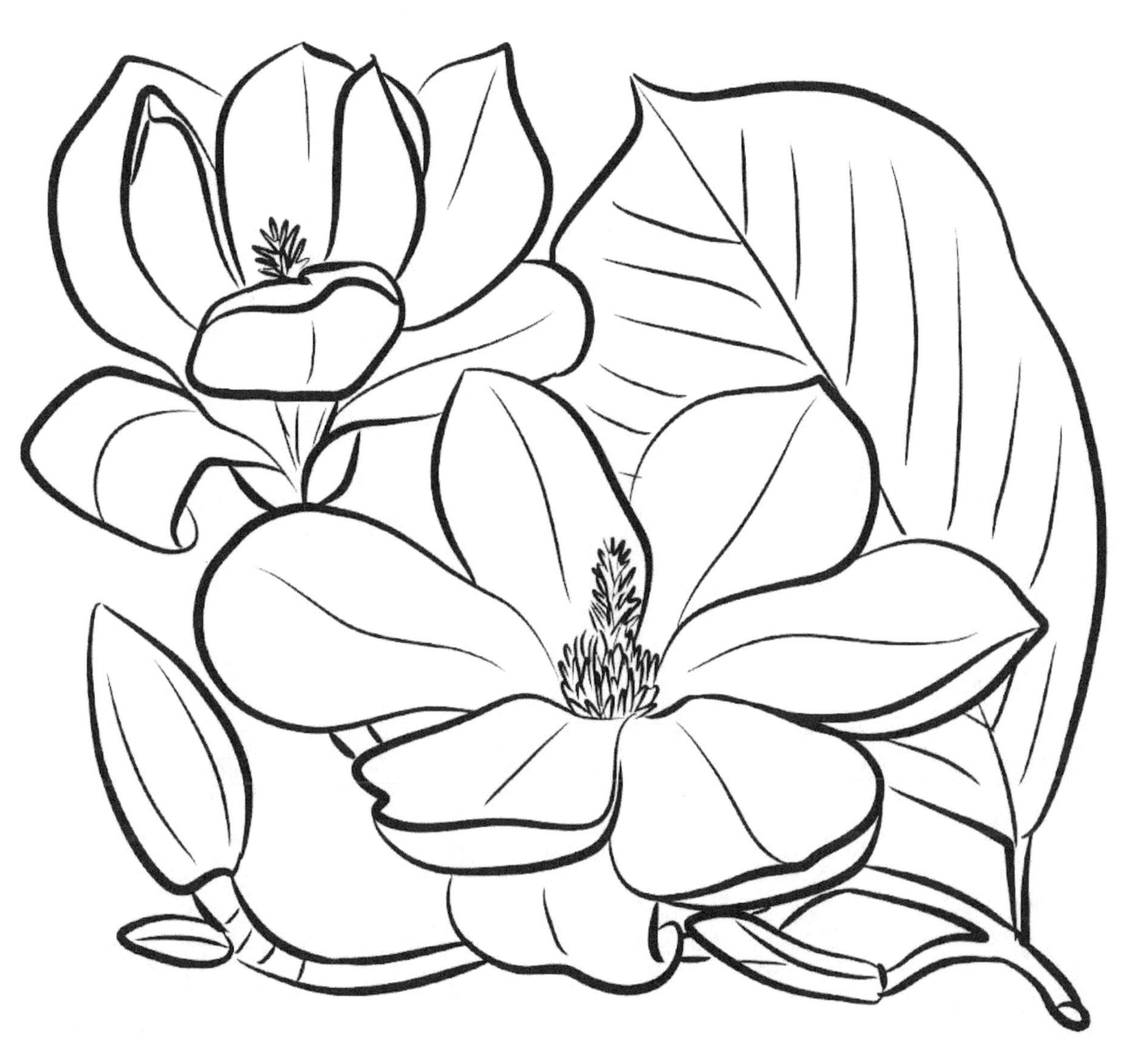

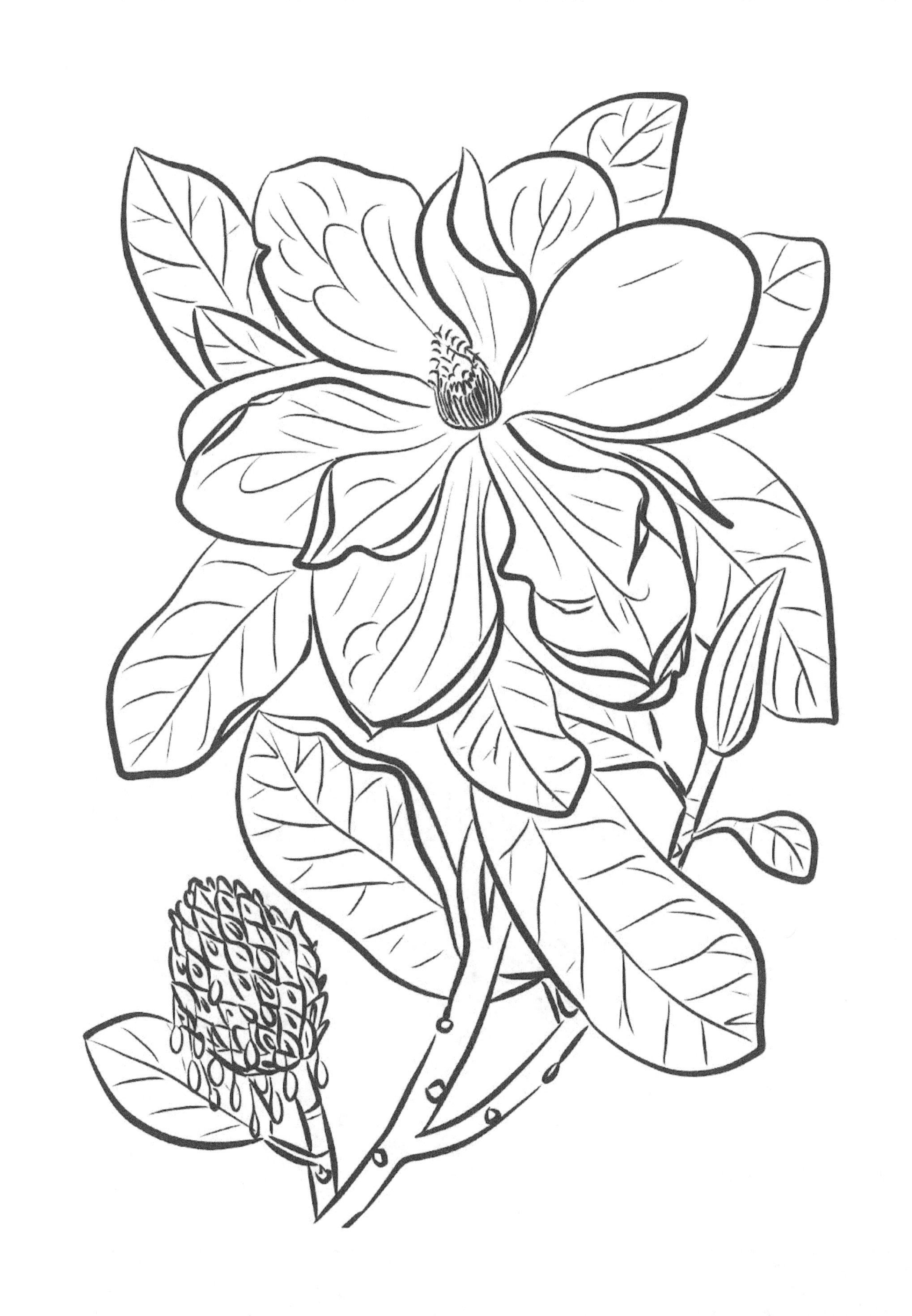

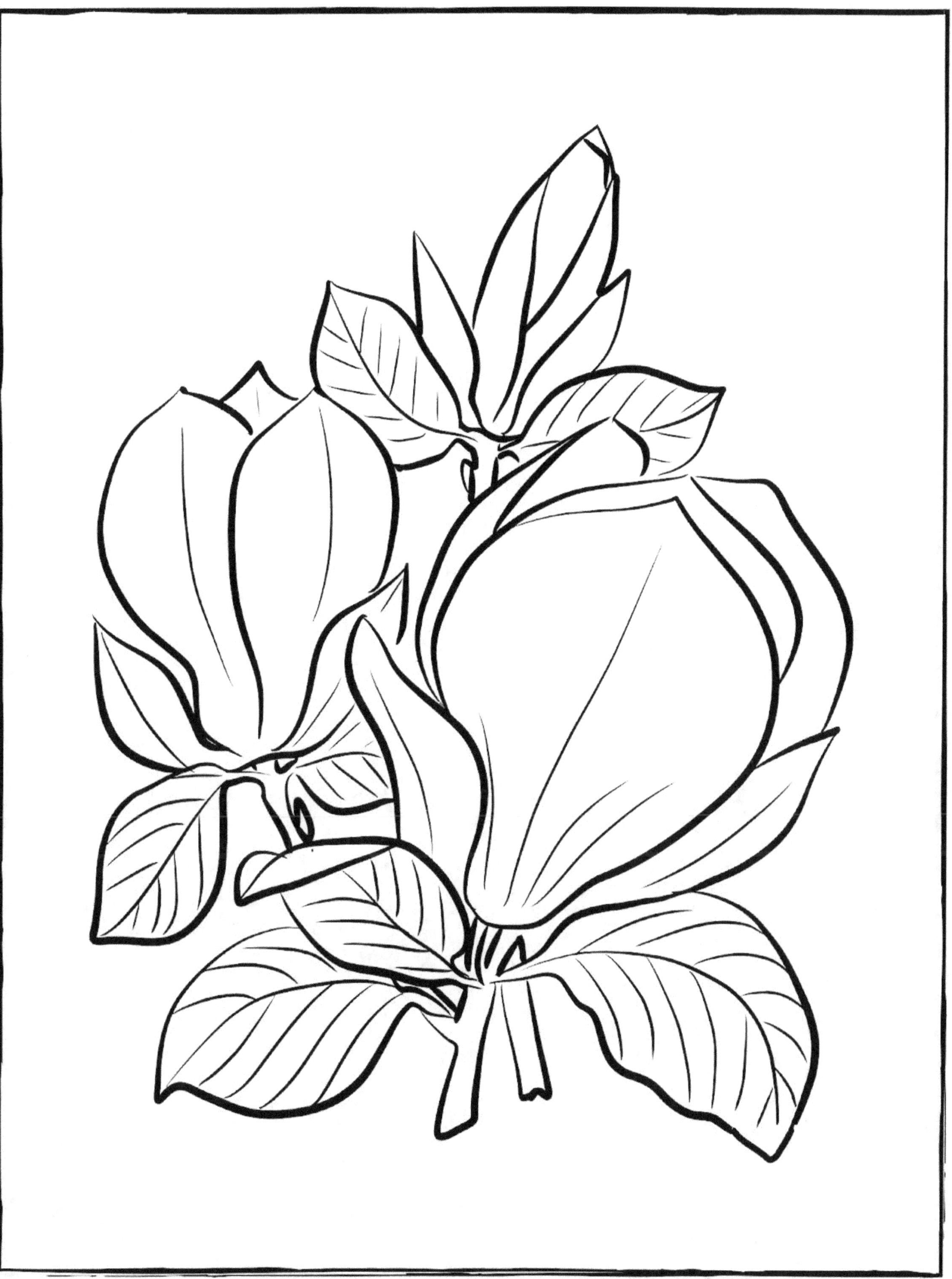

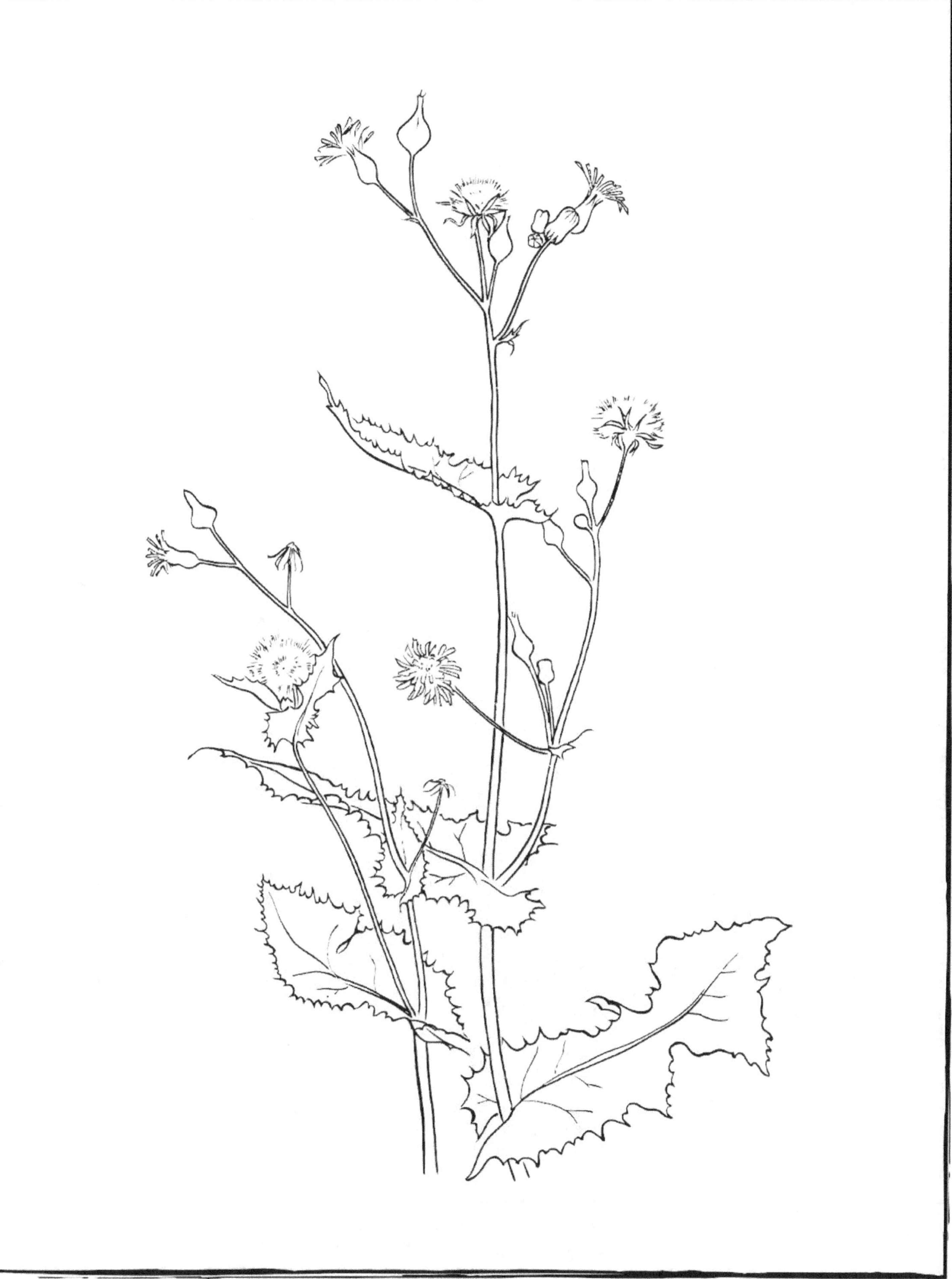

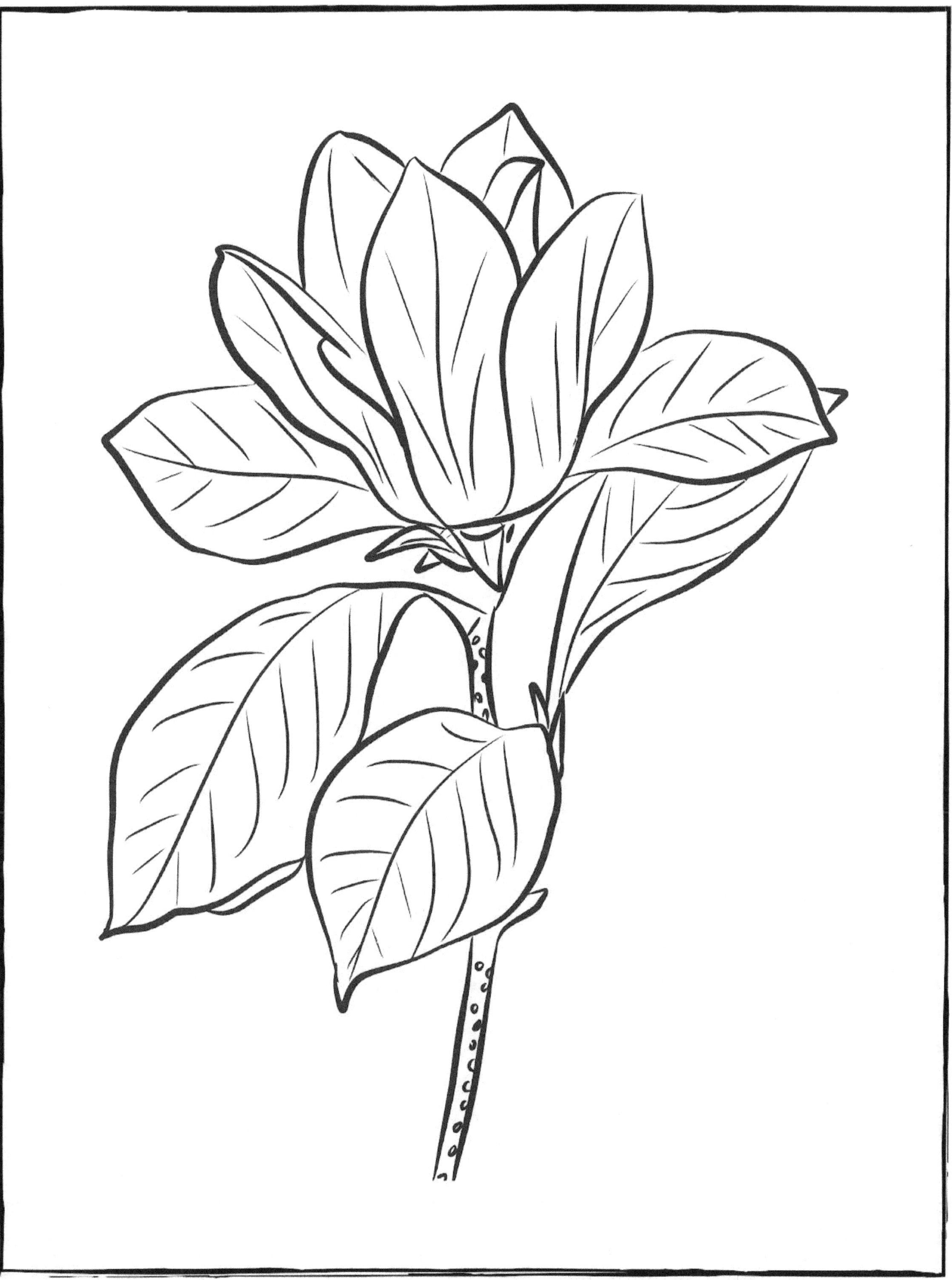

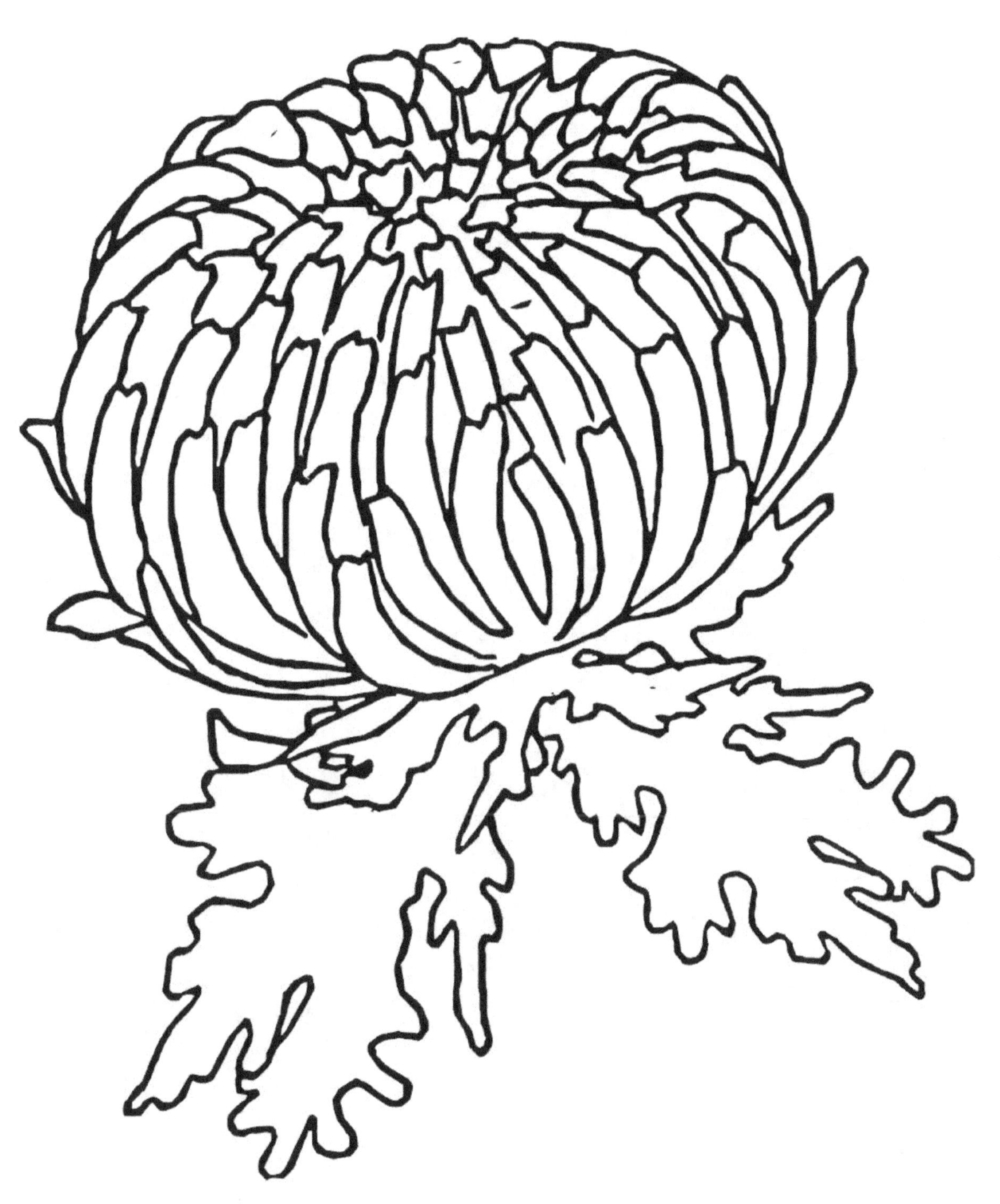

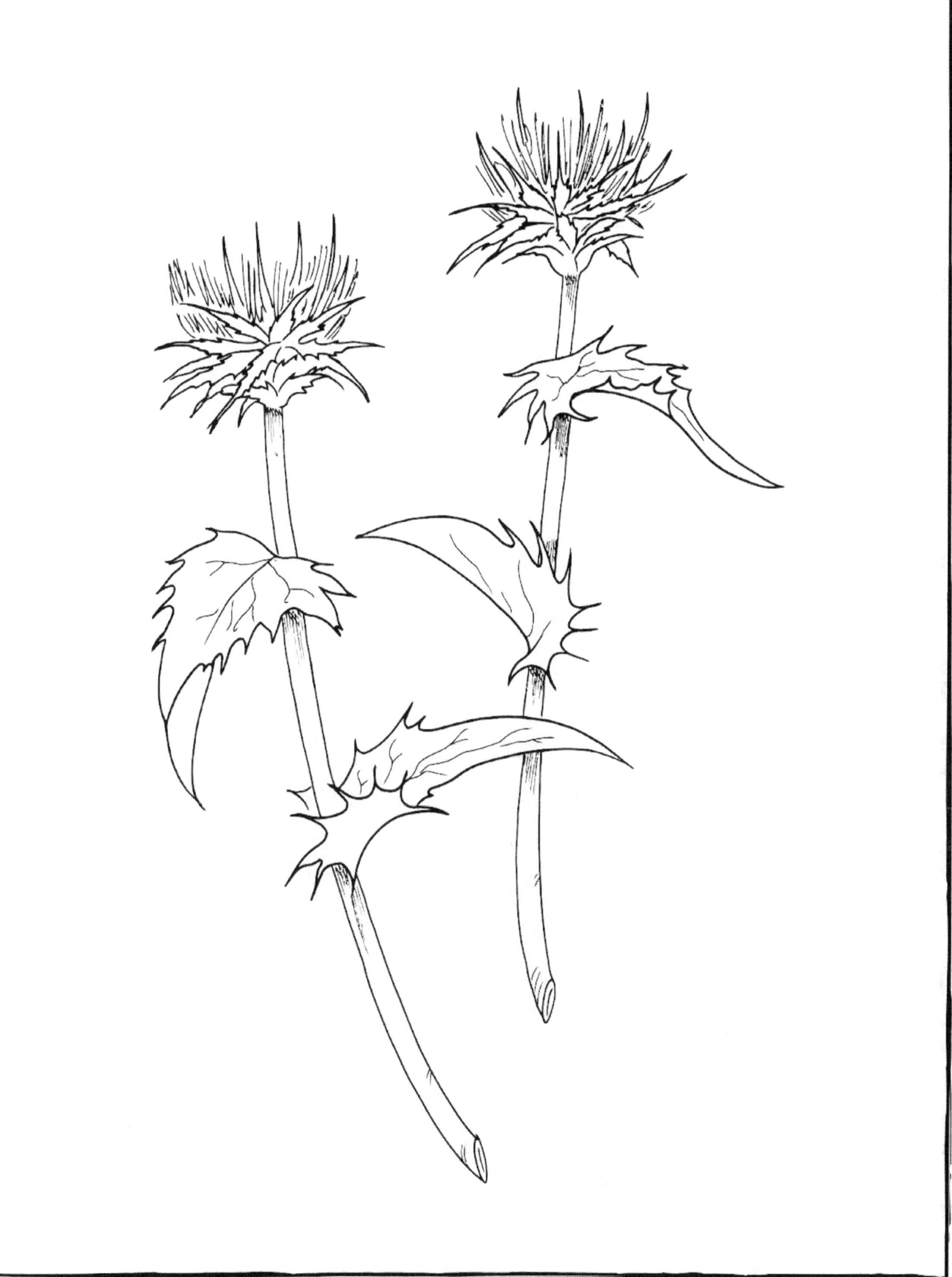

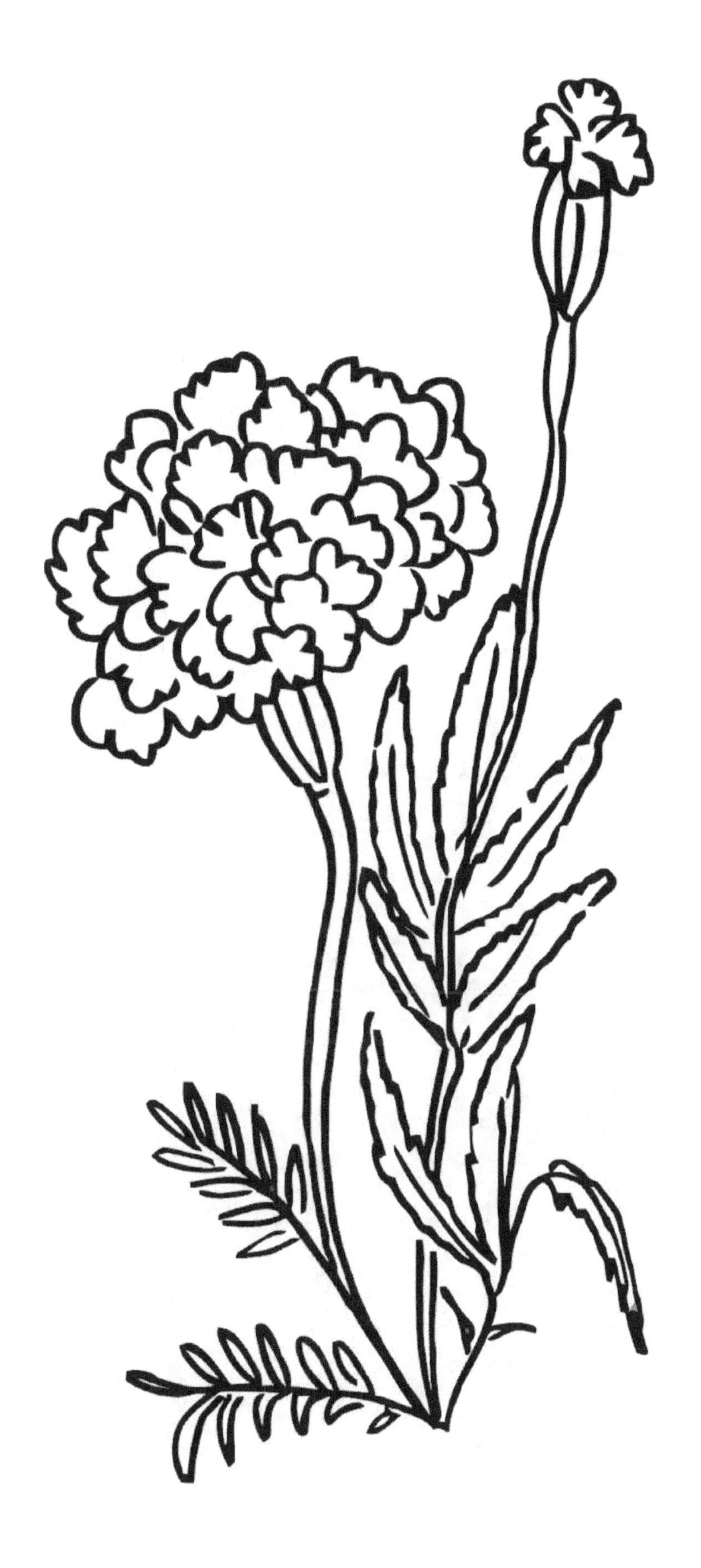

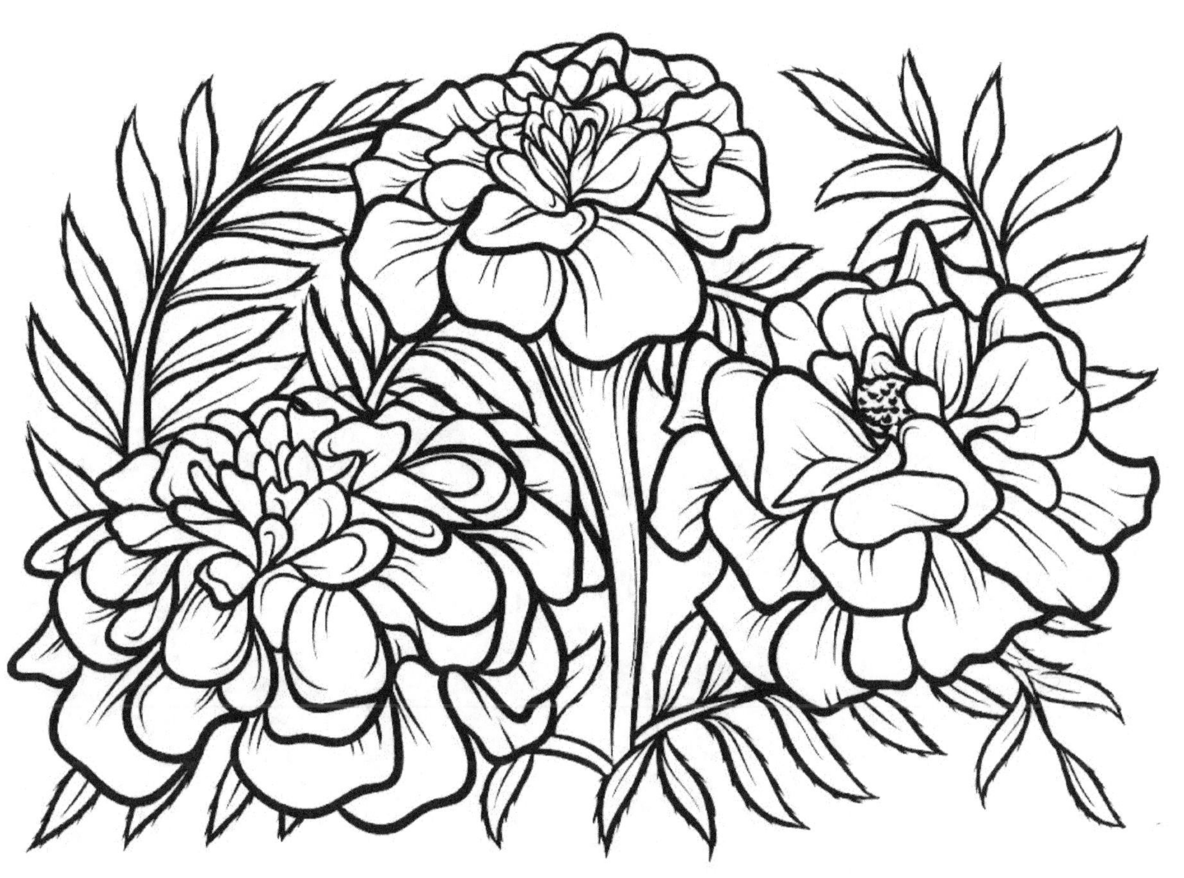

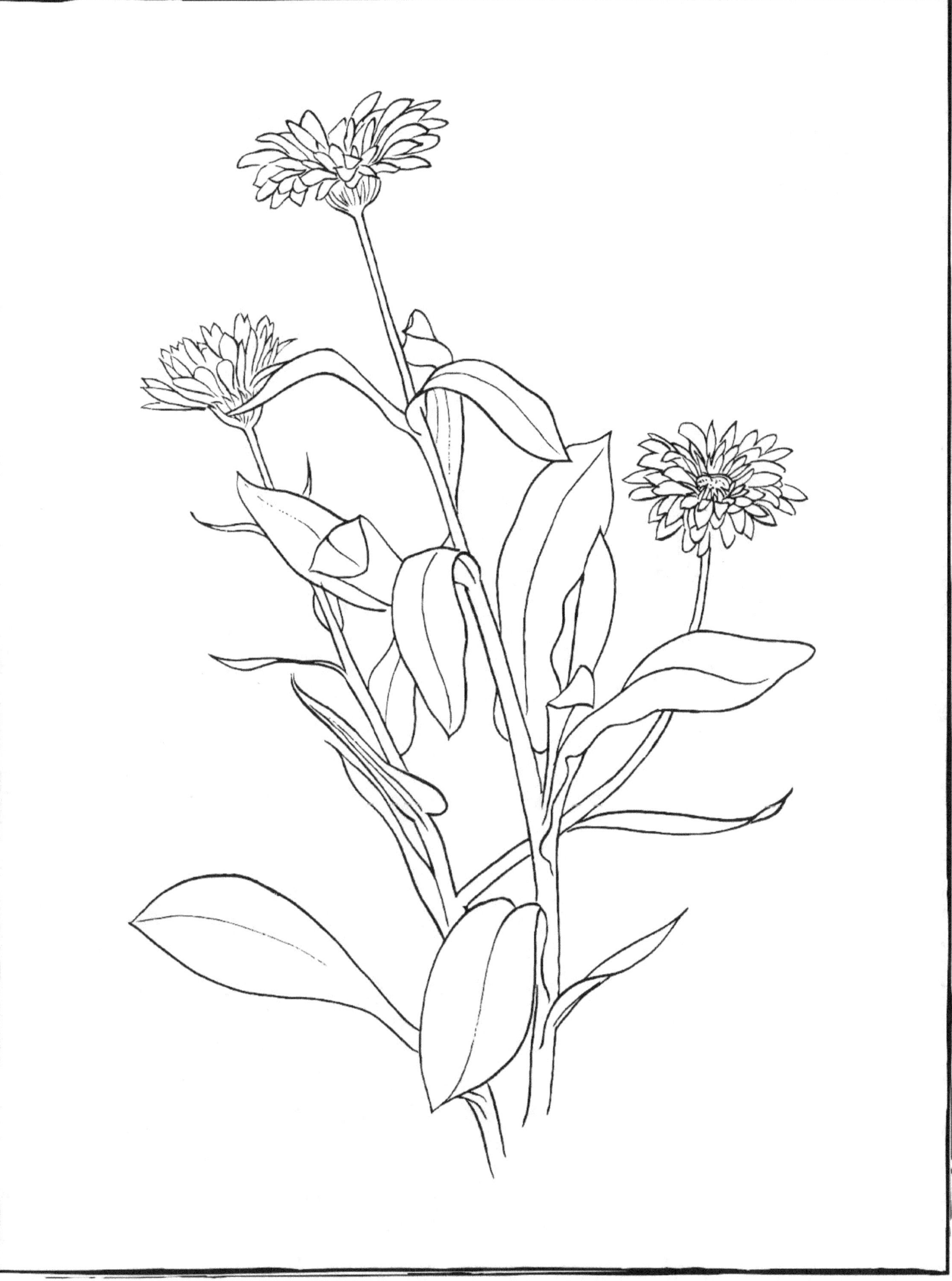

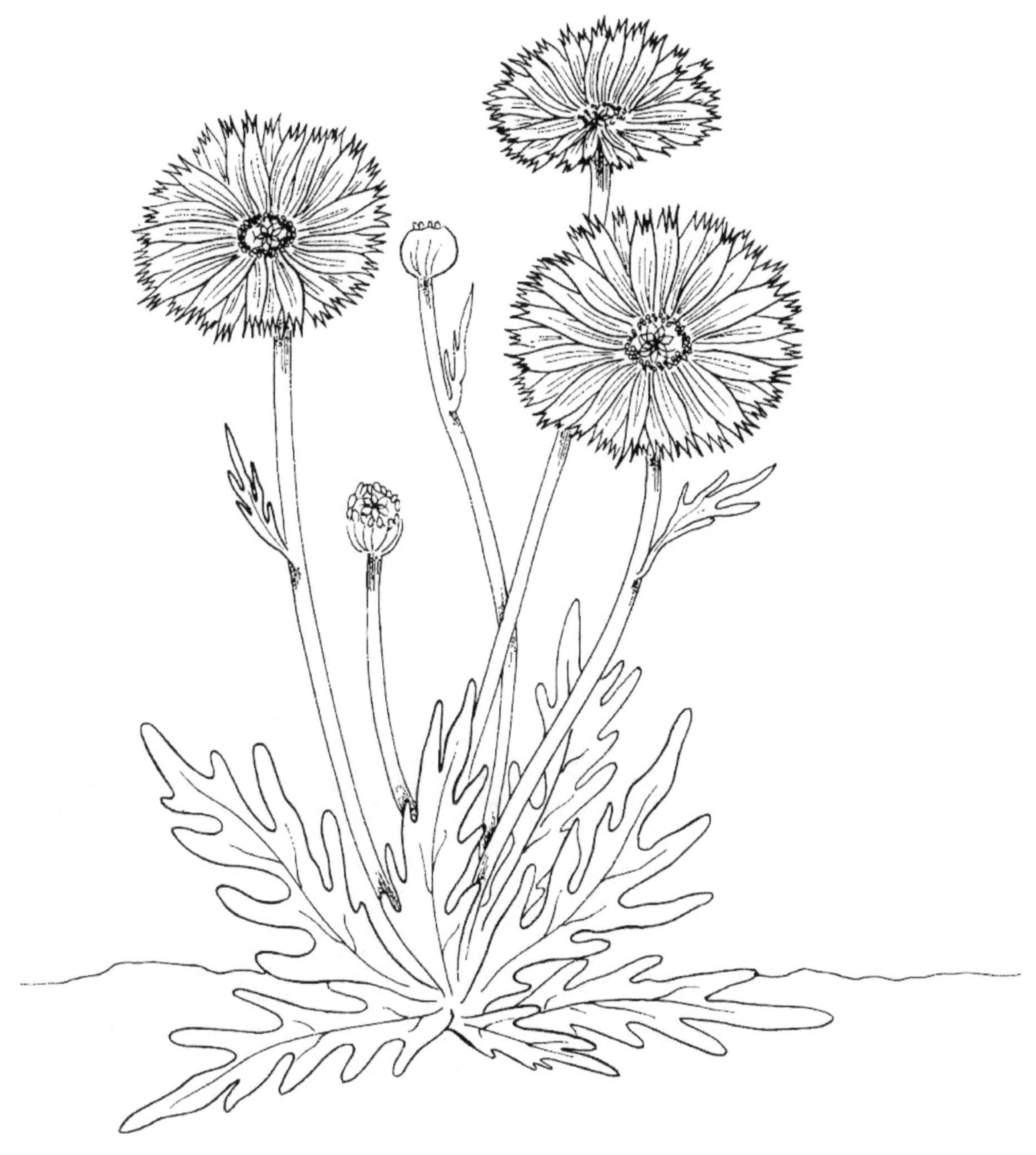

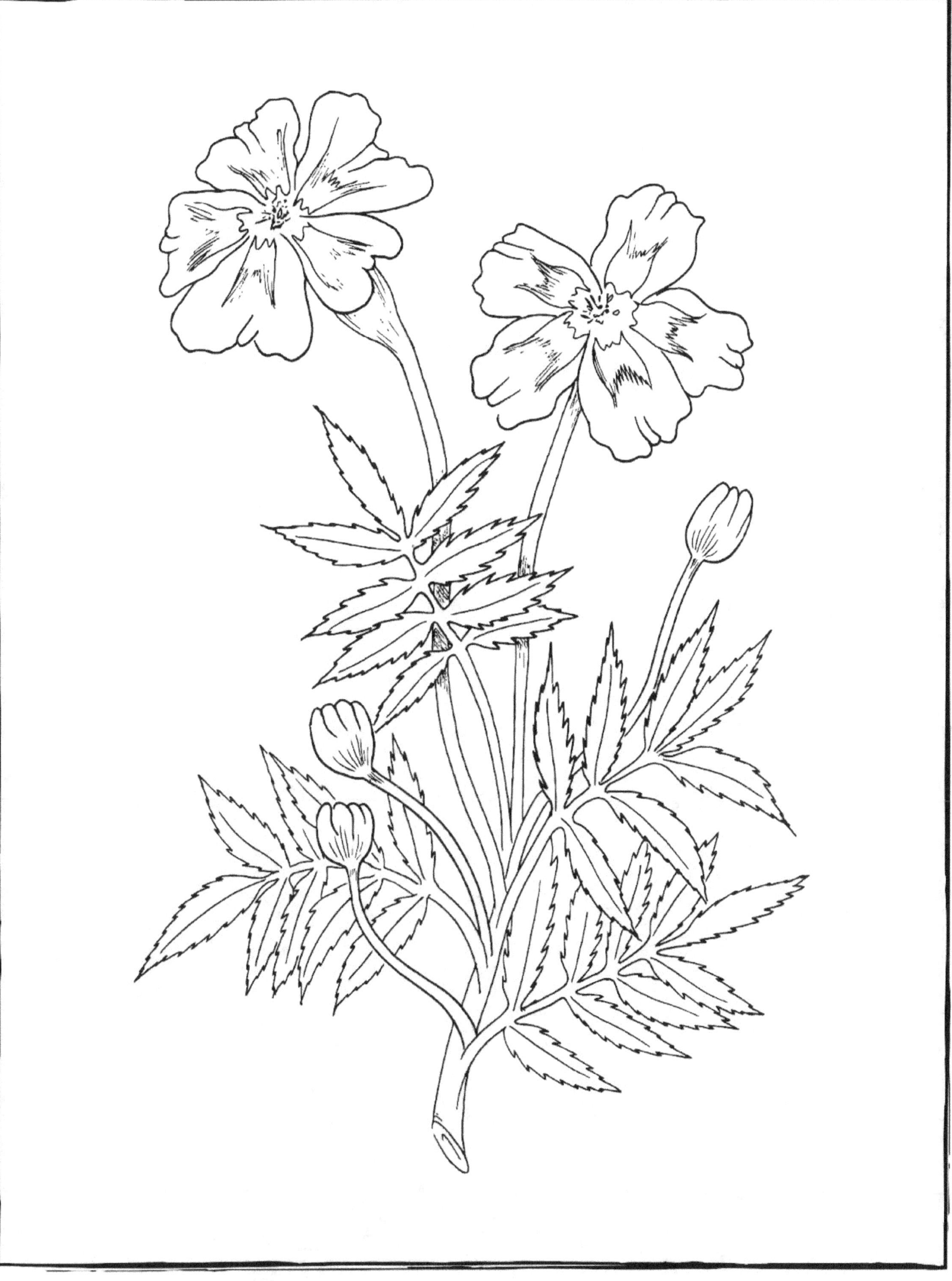

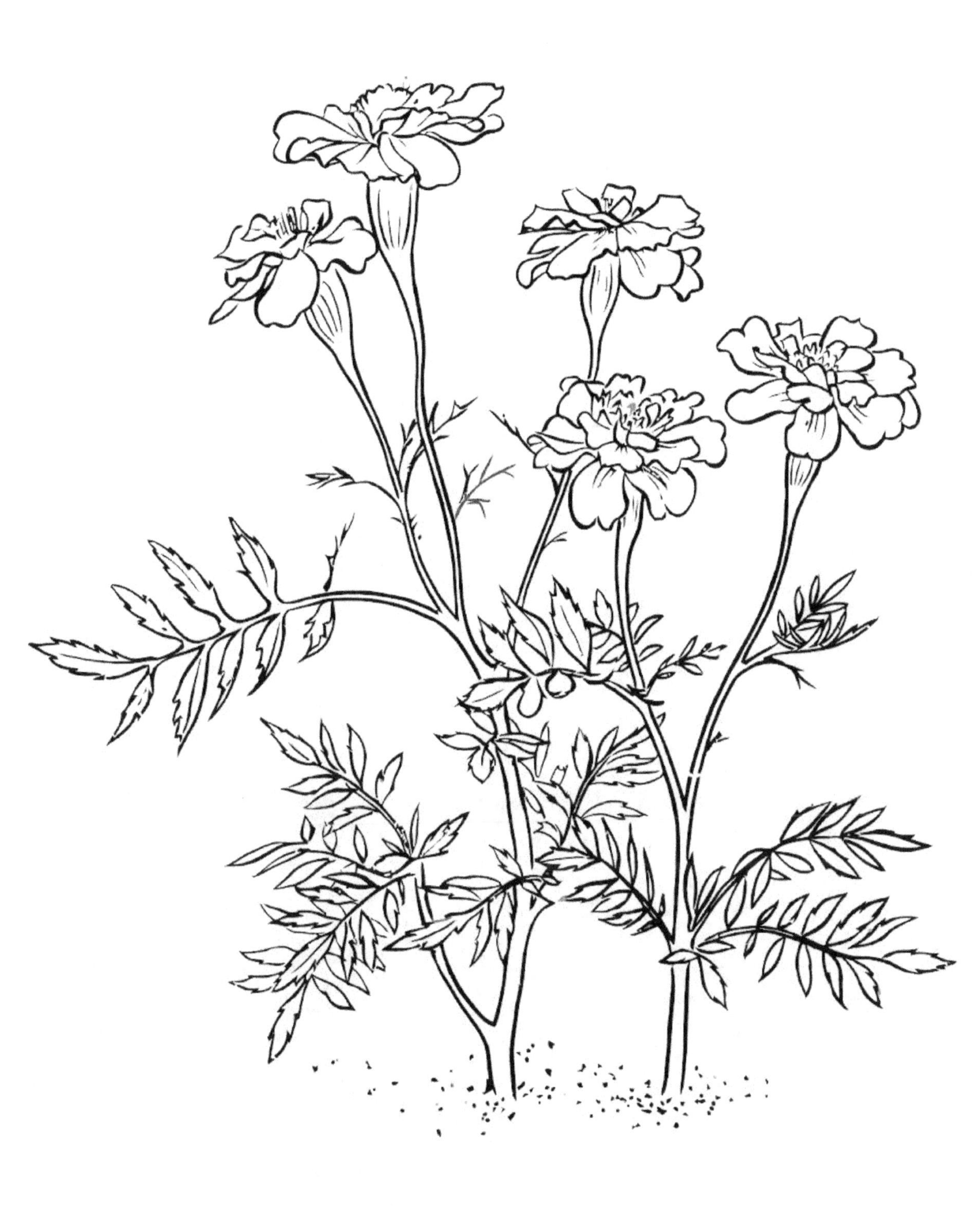

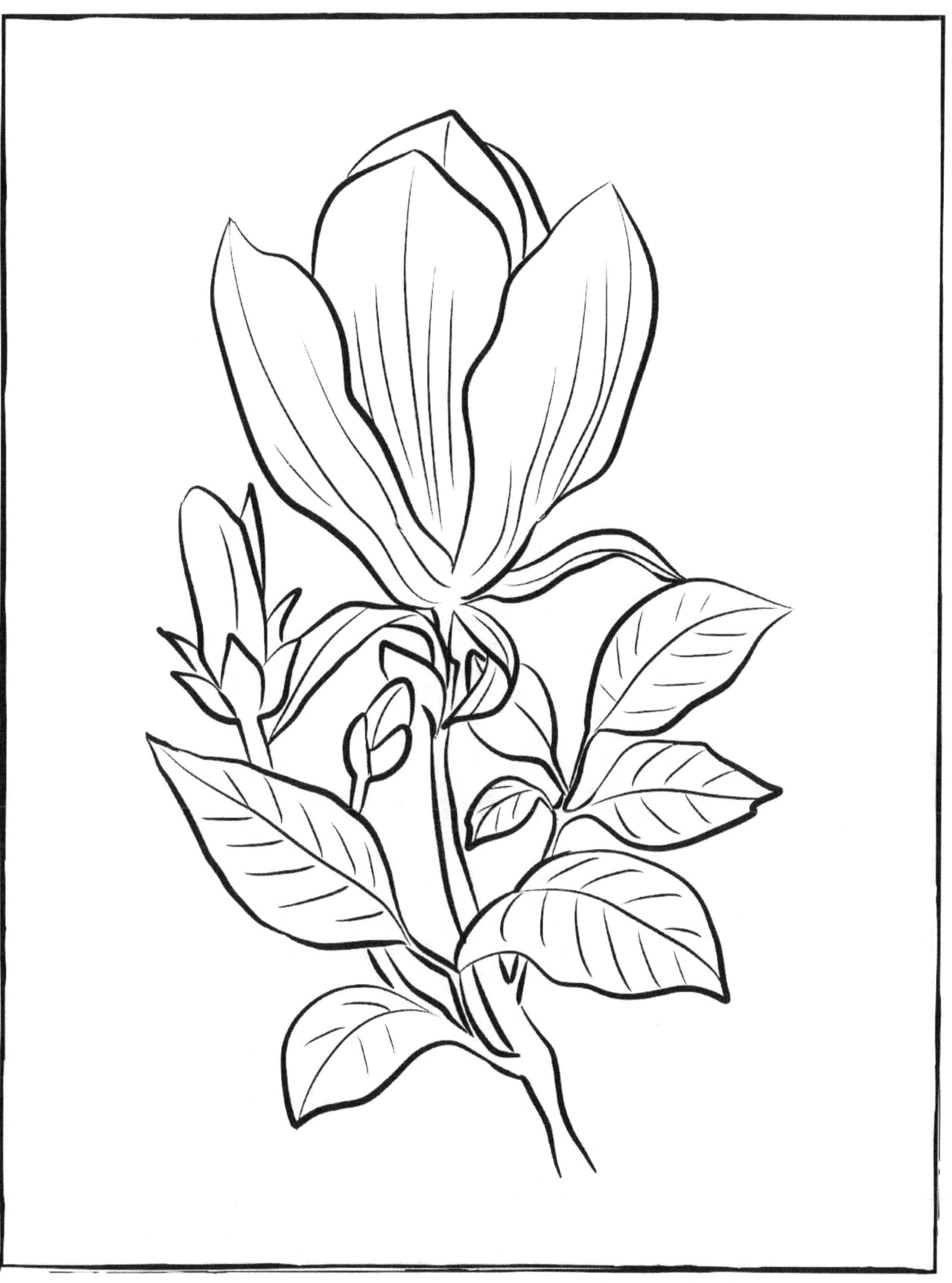

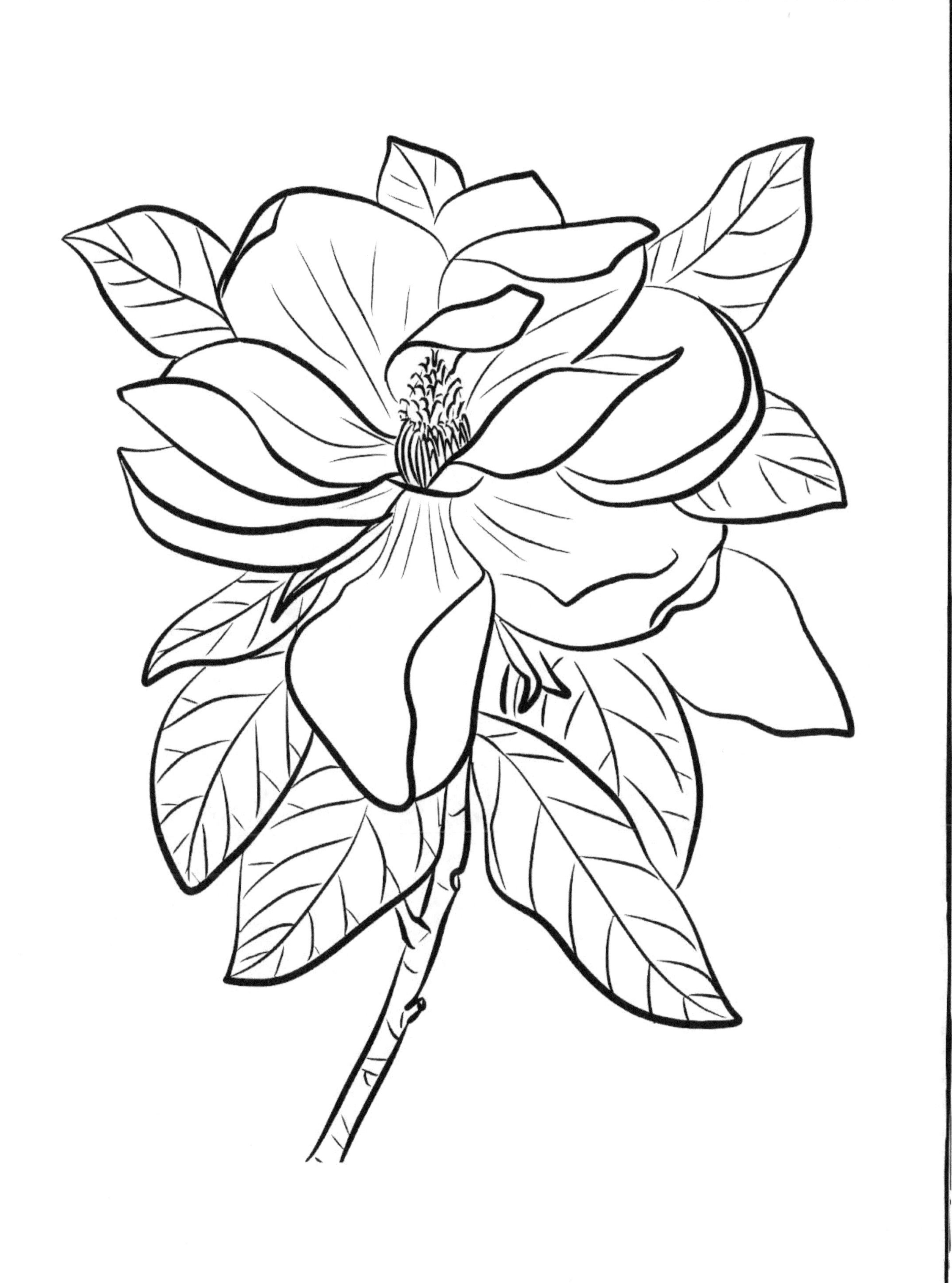

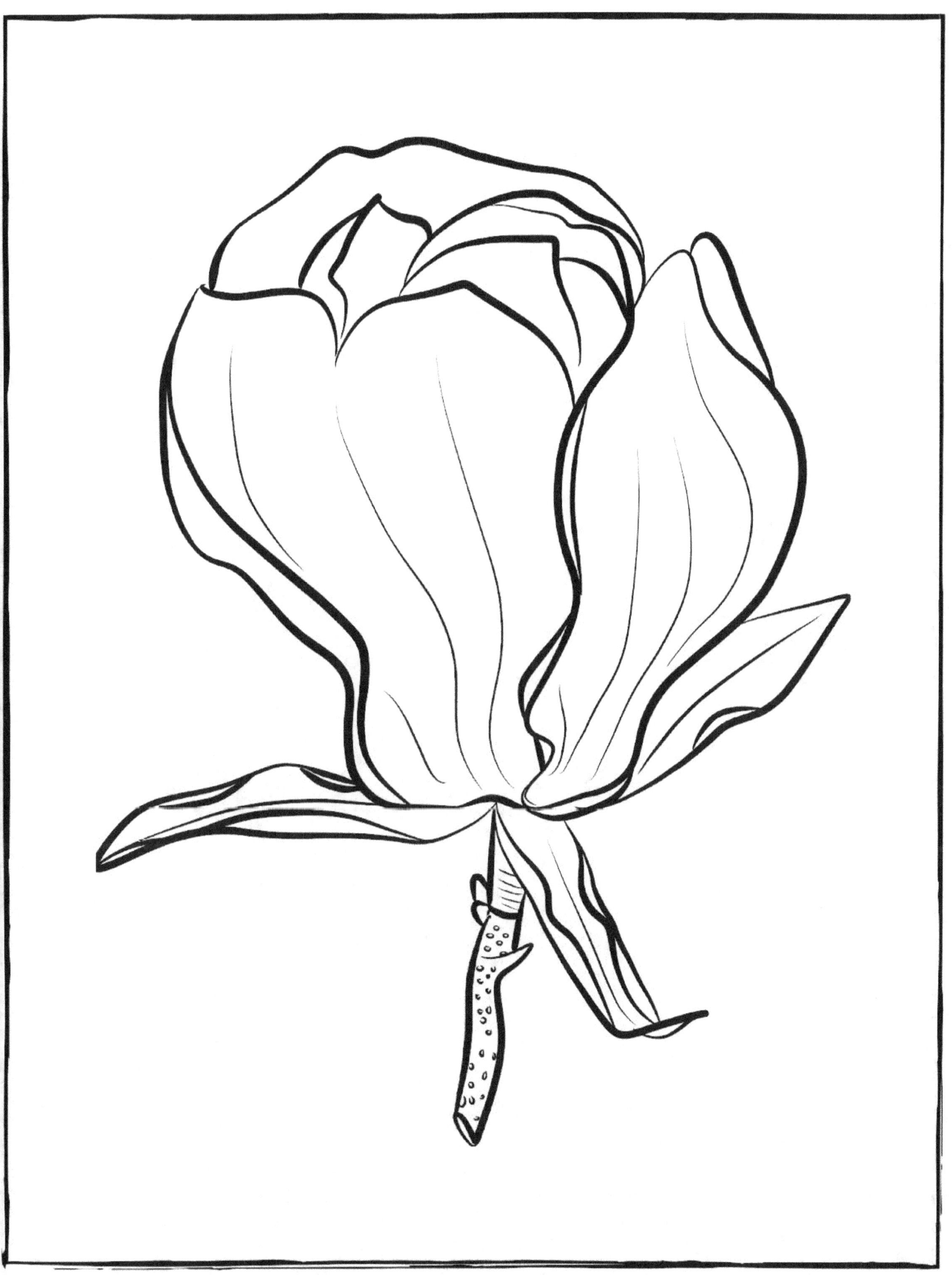

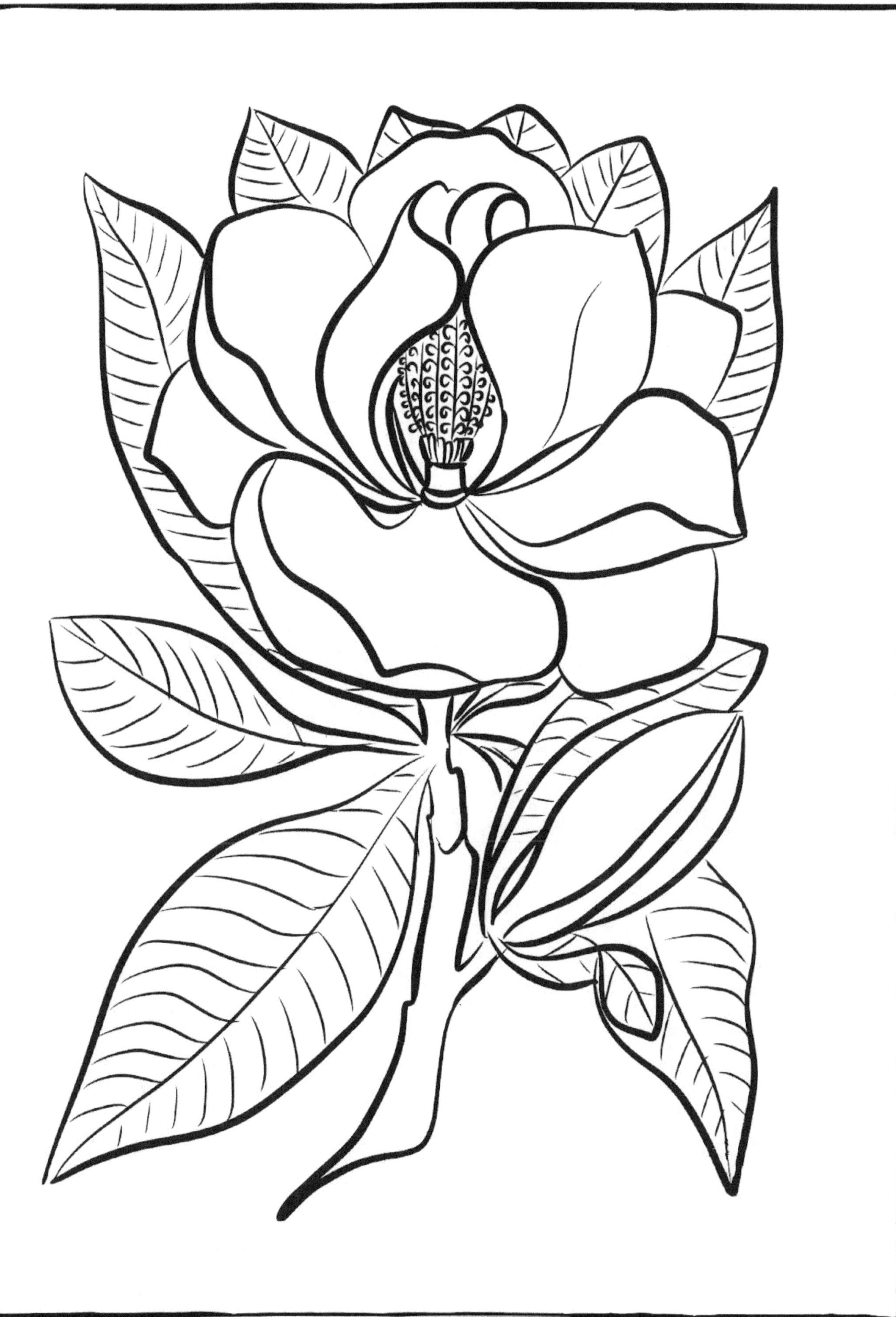

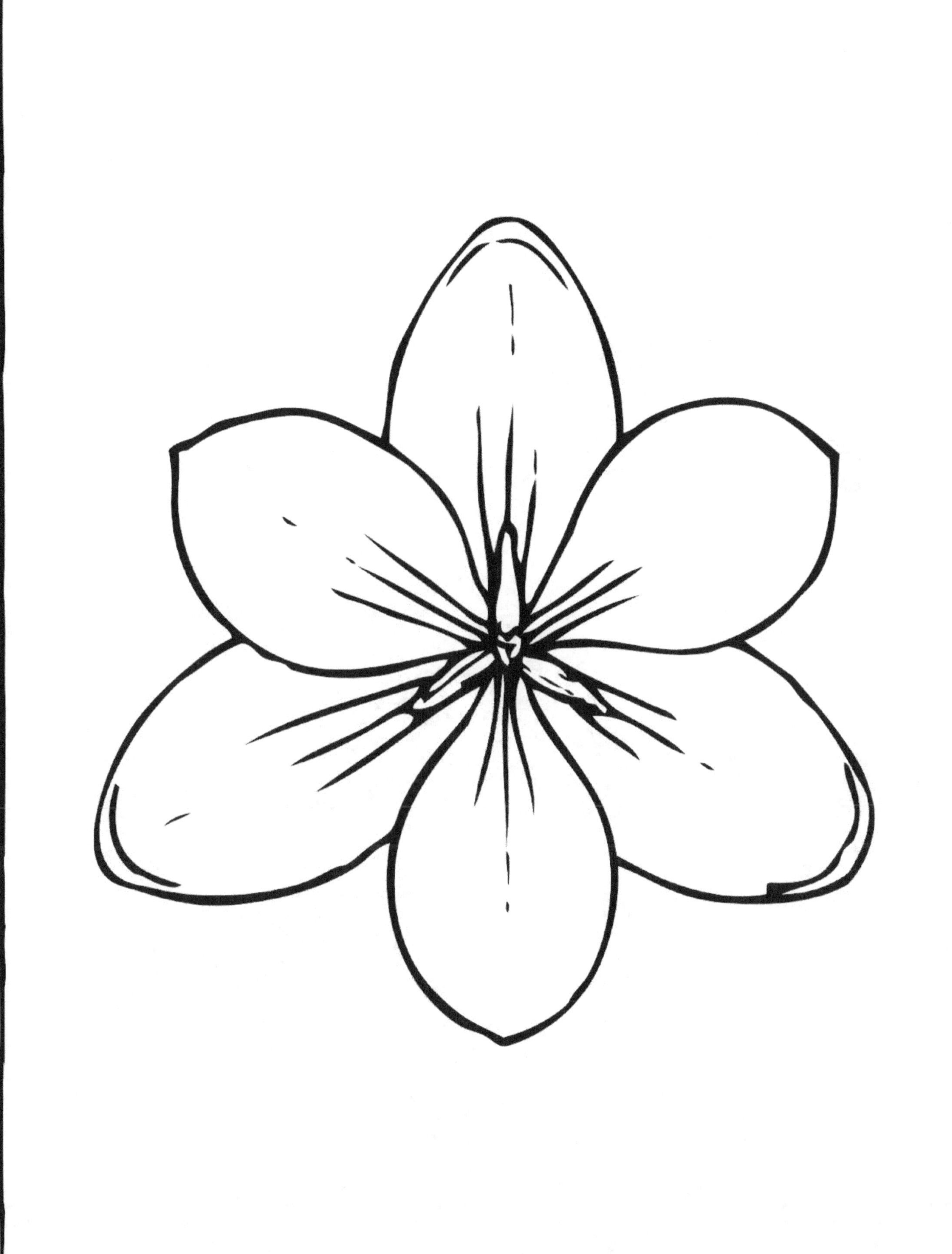

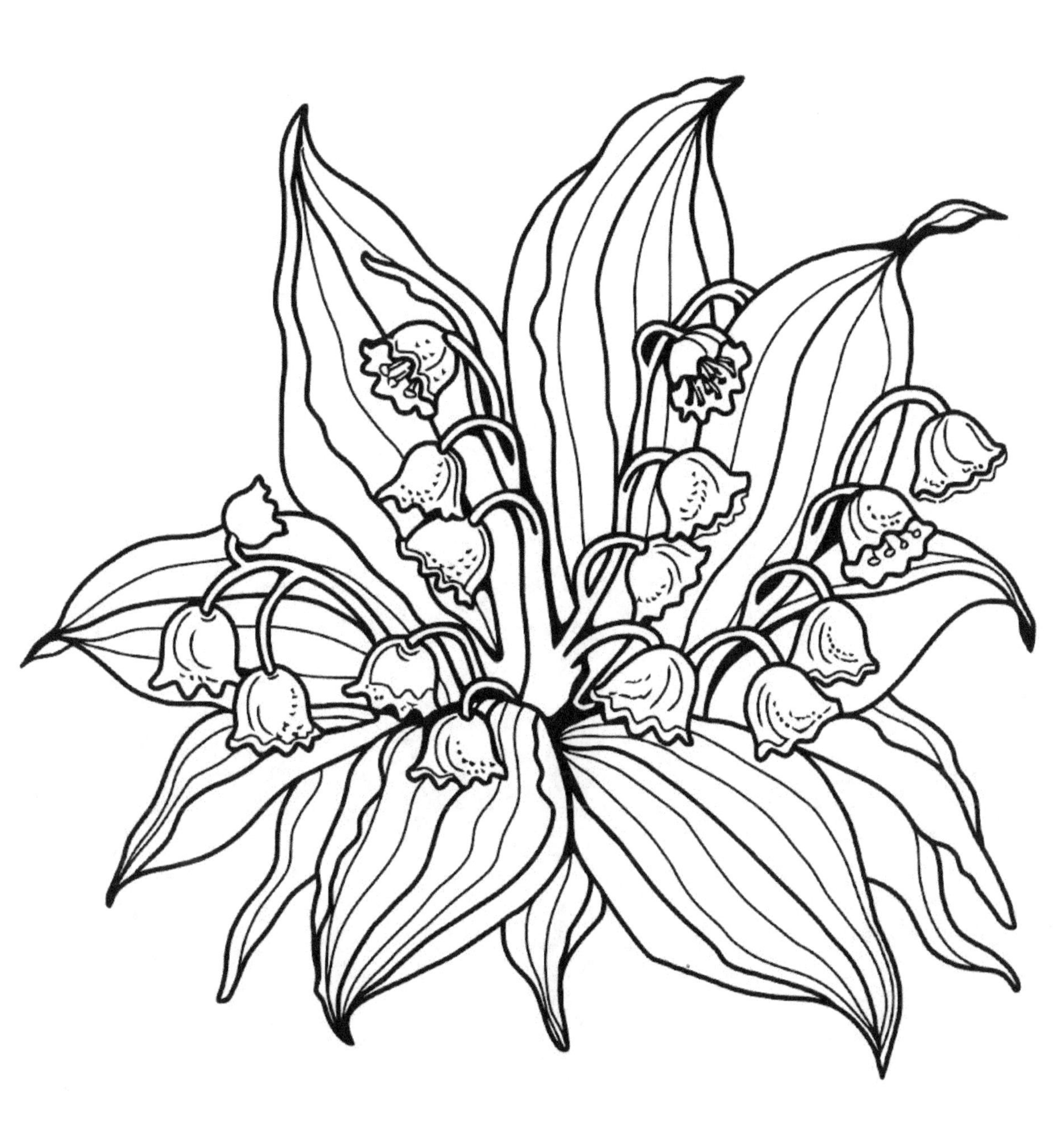

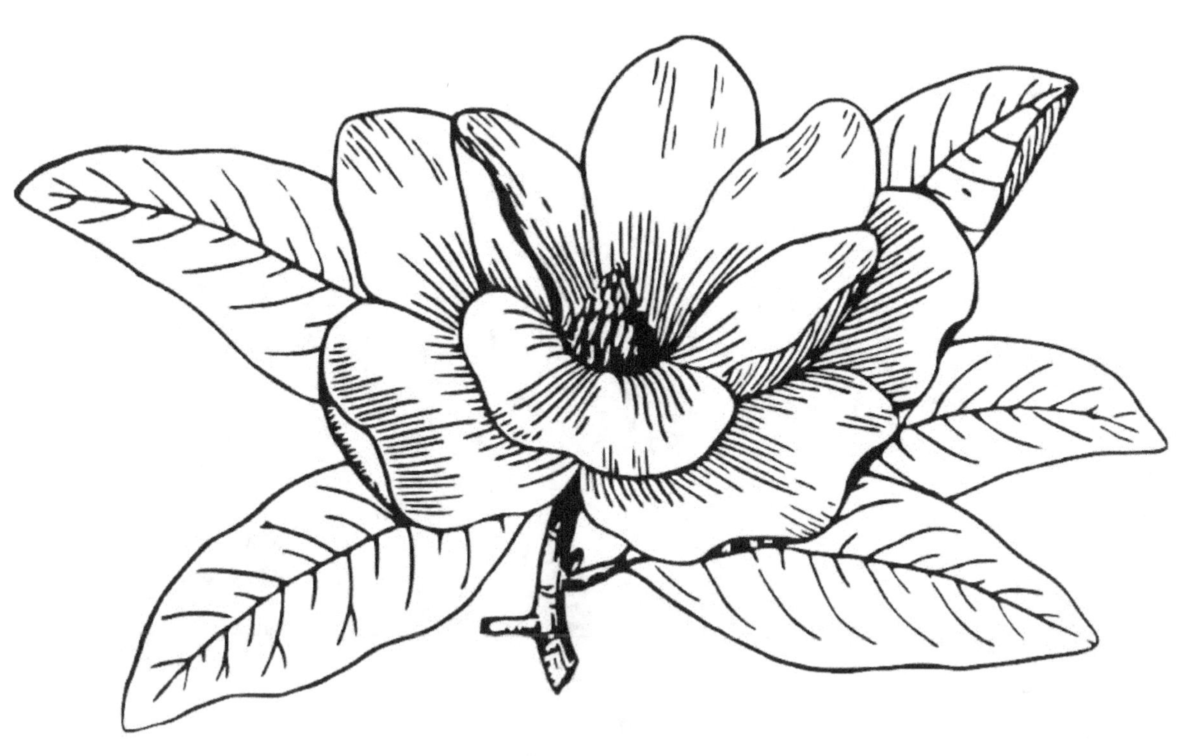

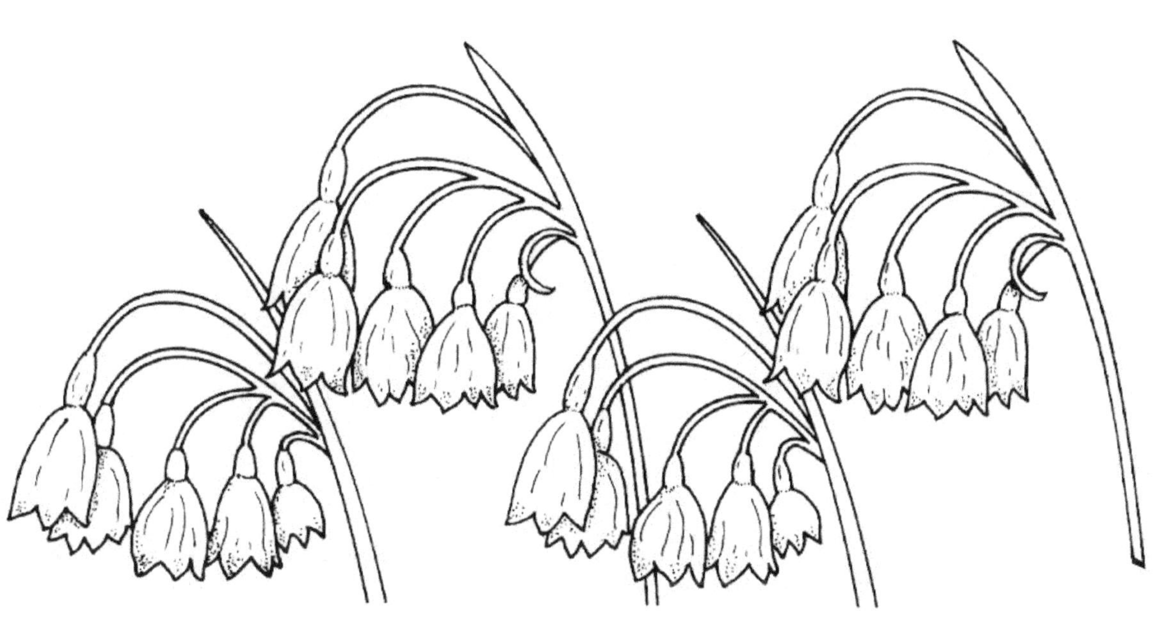

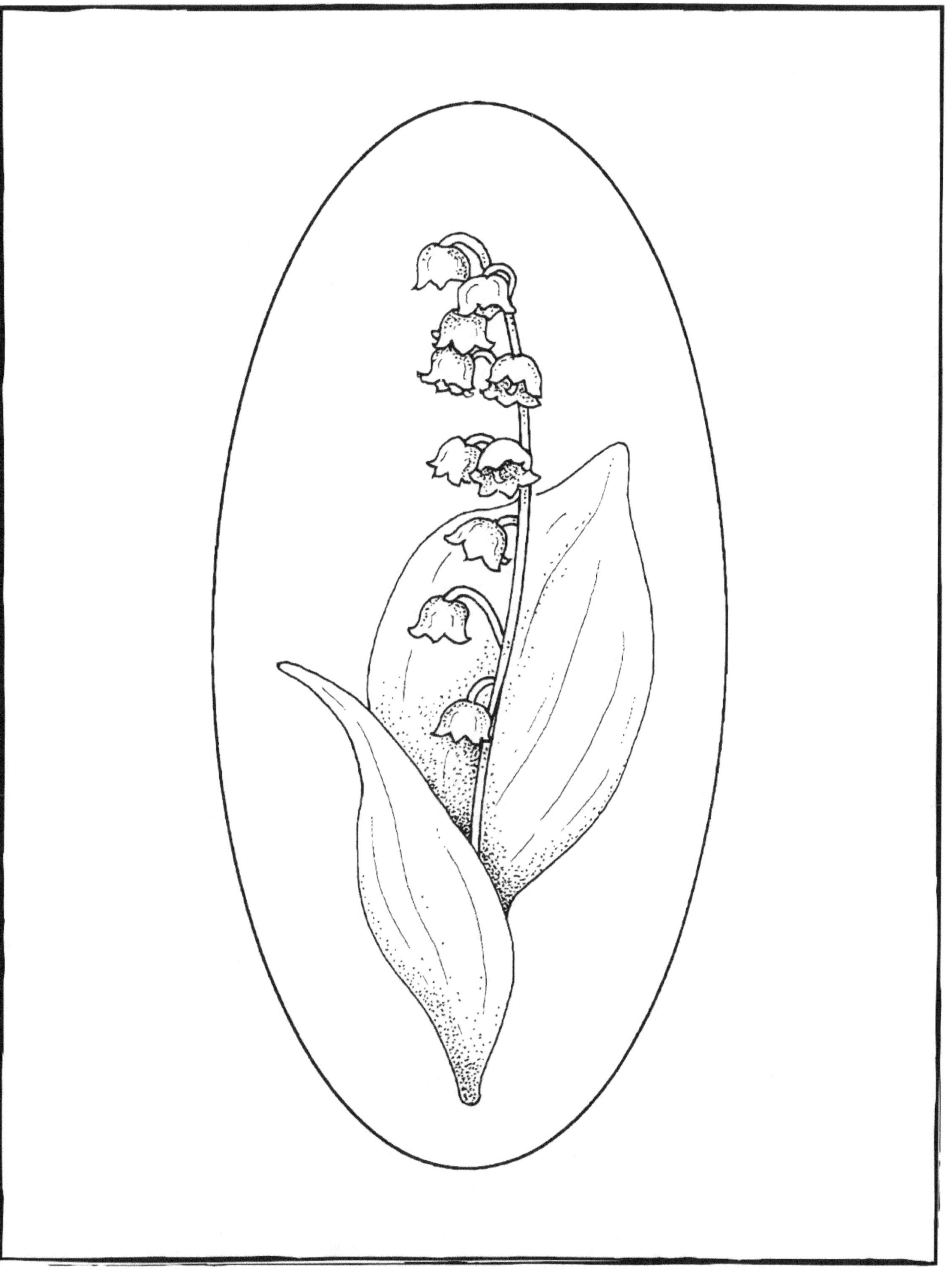

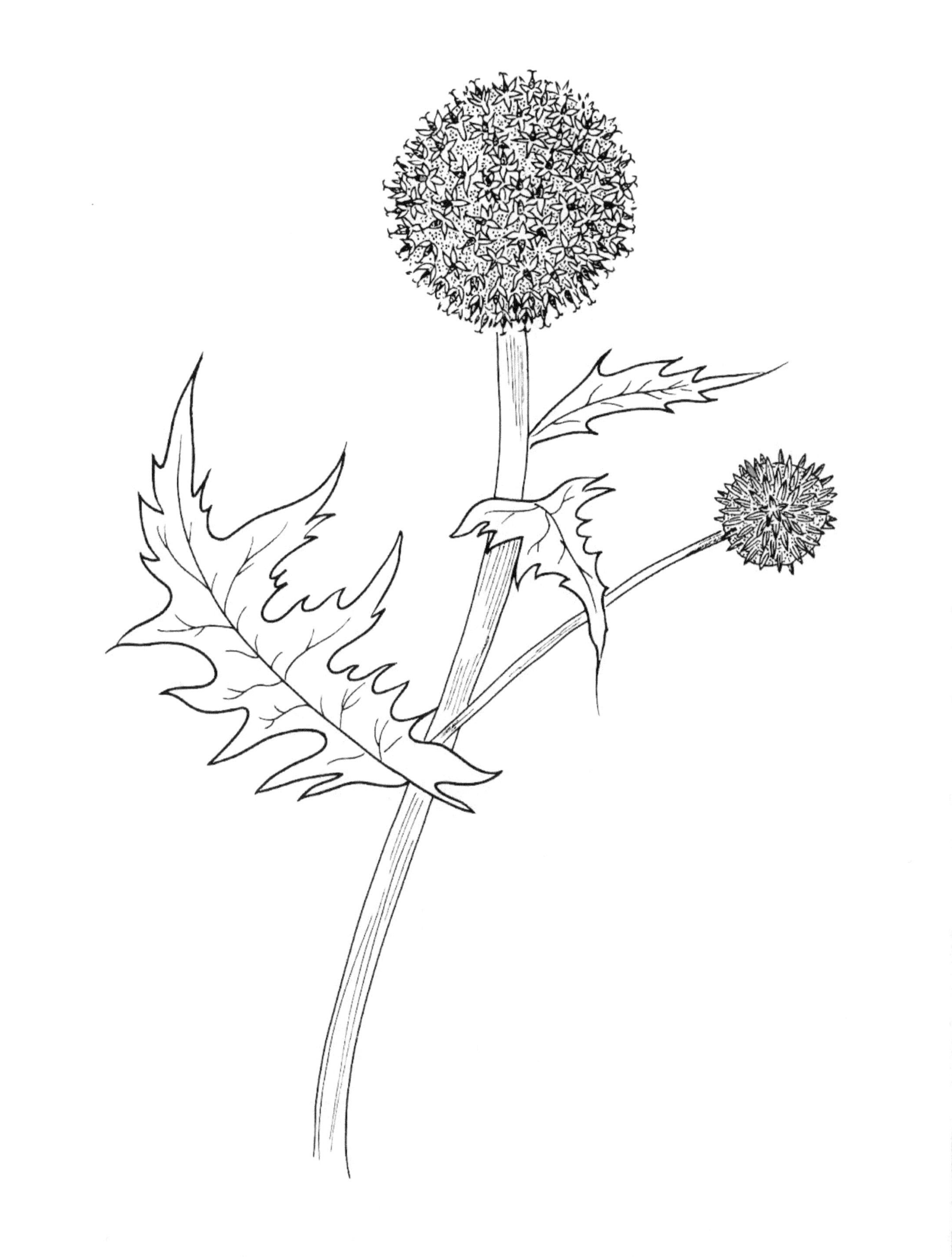

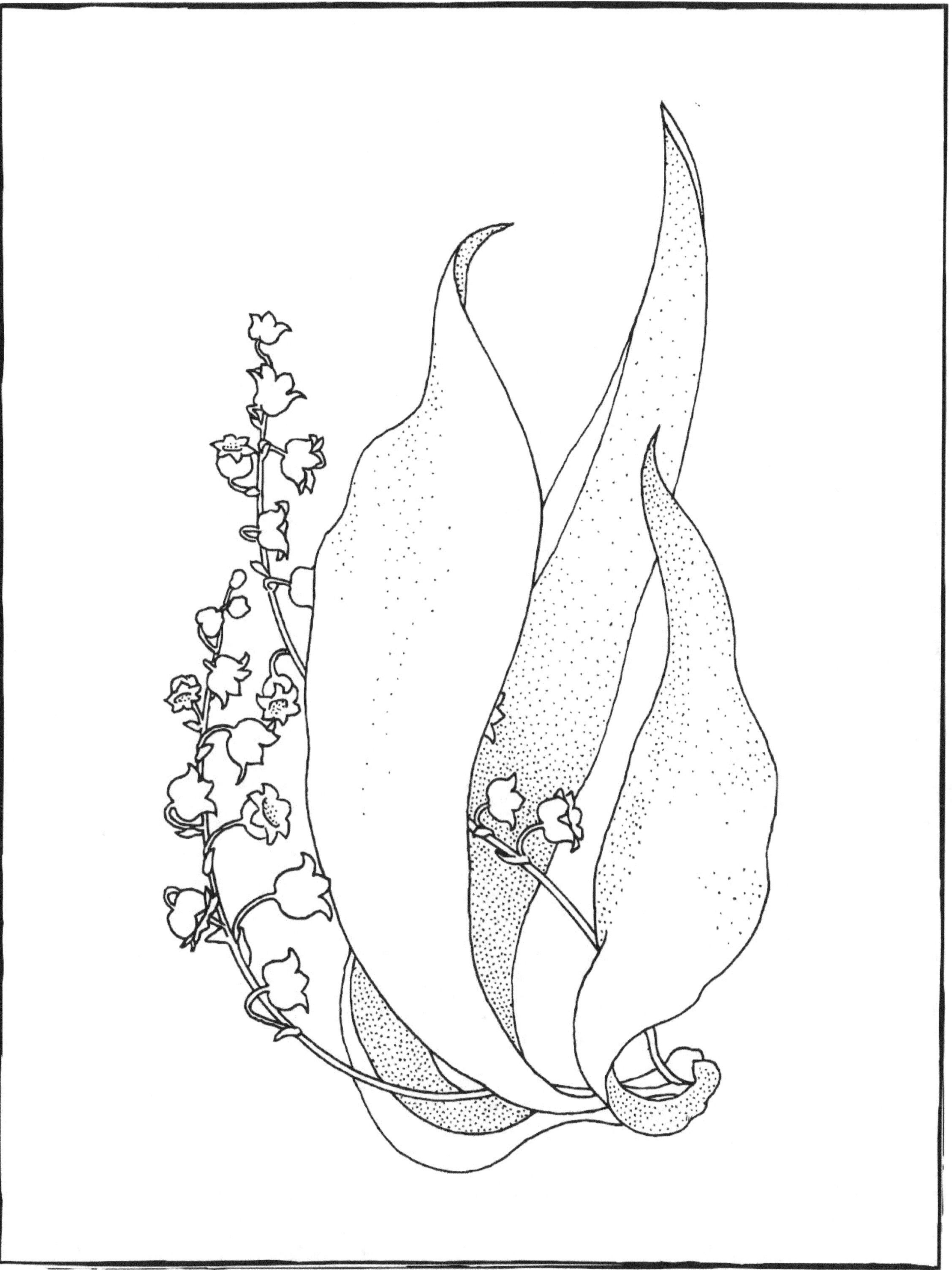

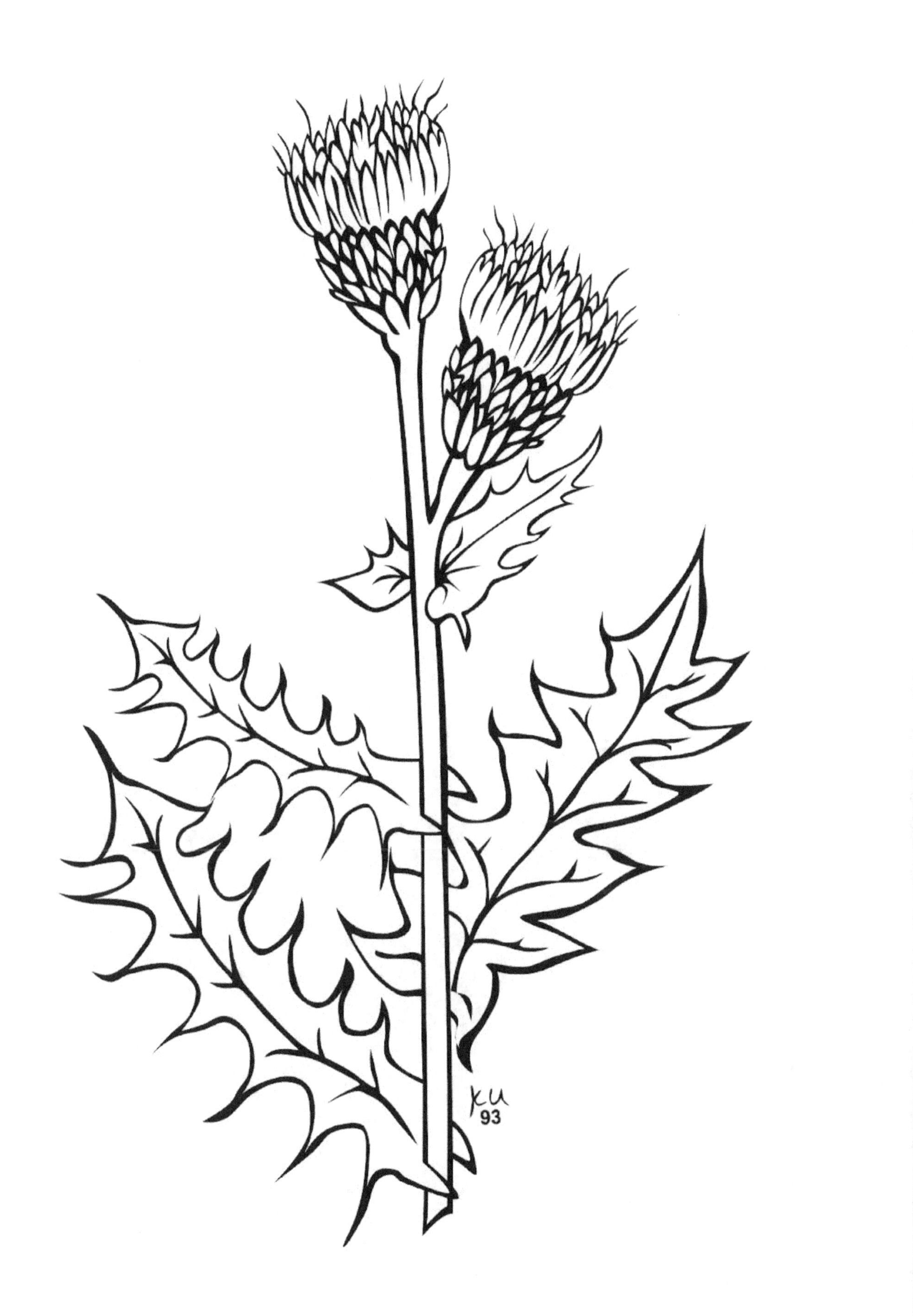

KU
93

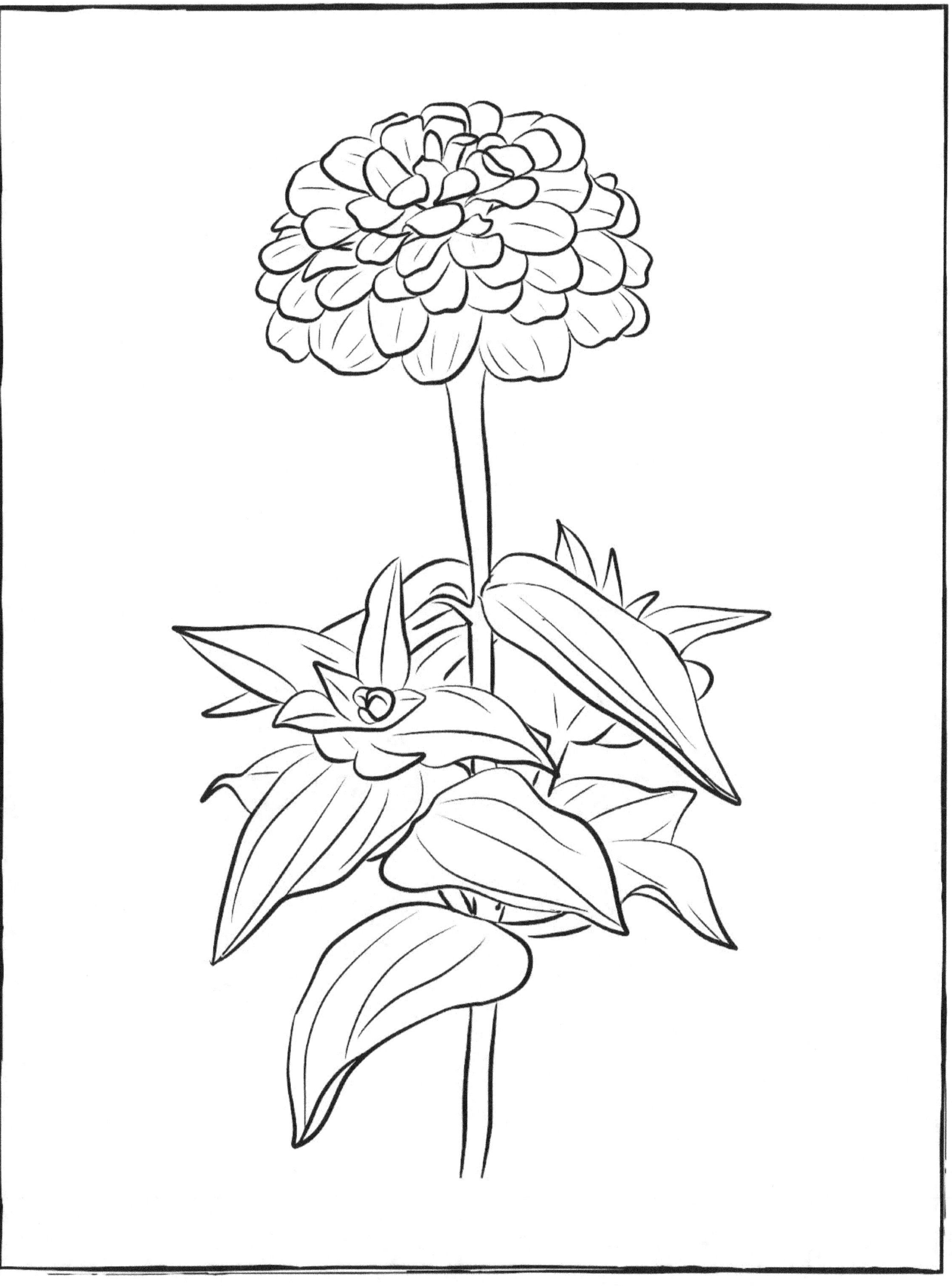

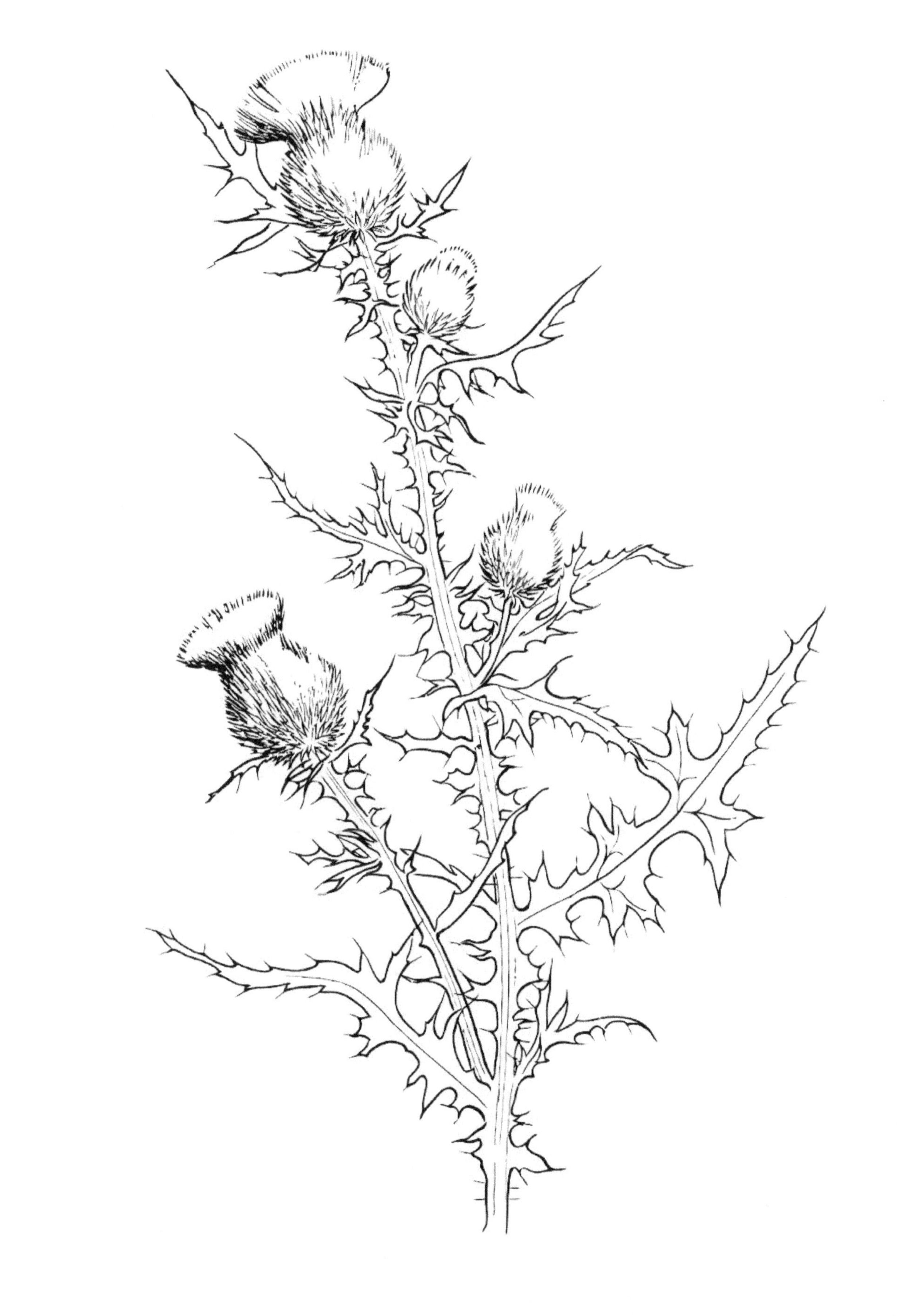

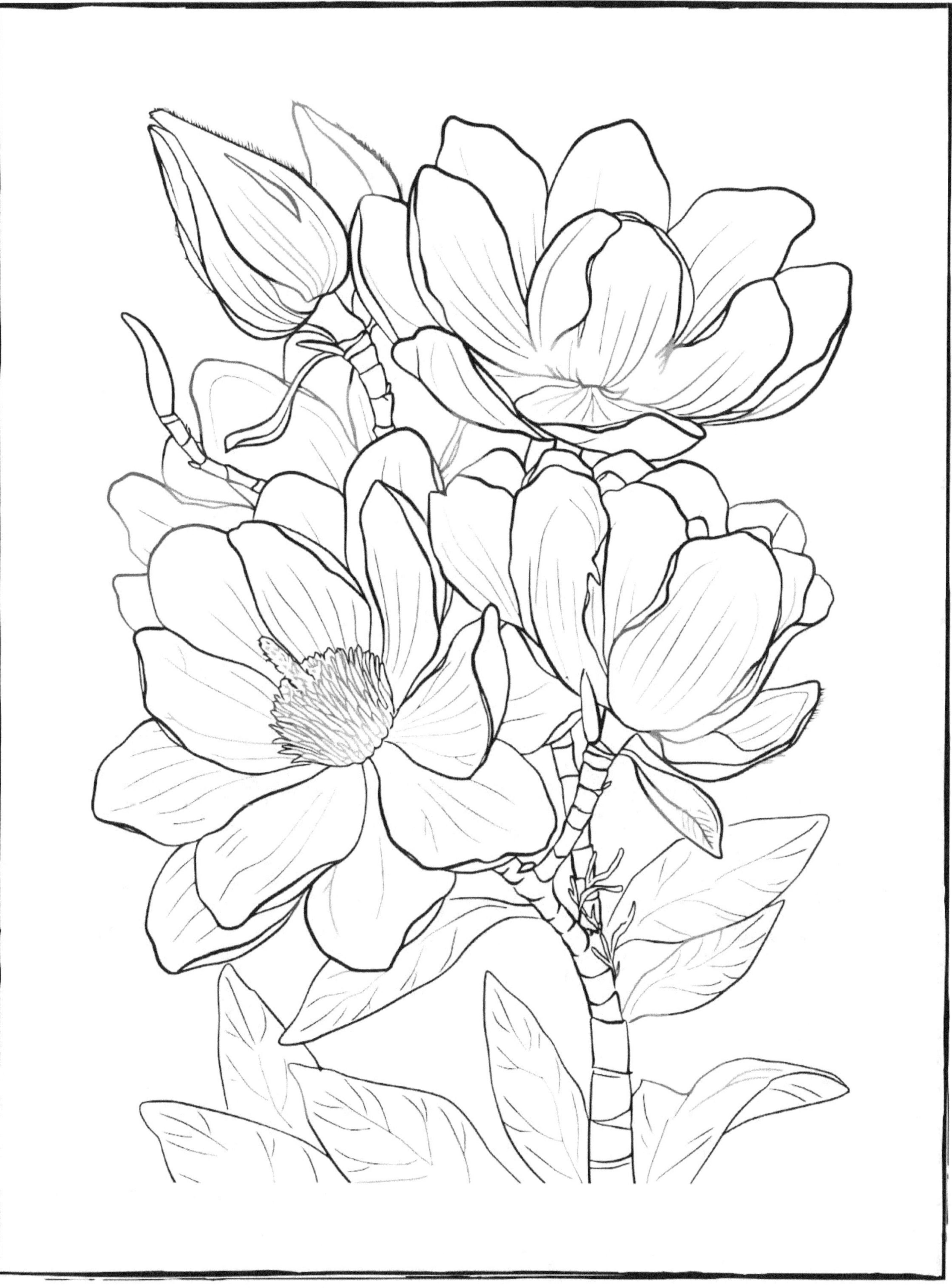

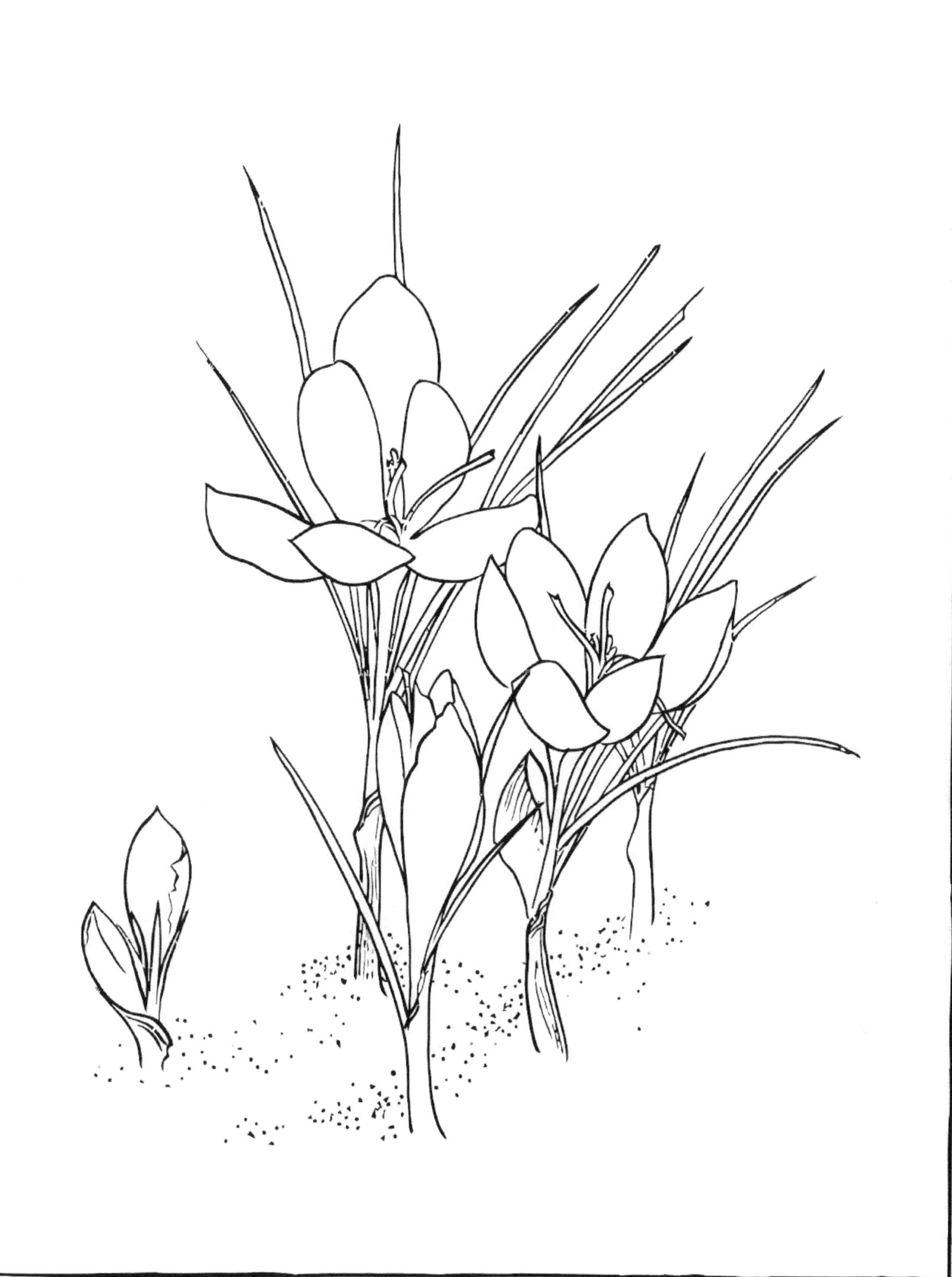

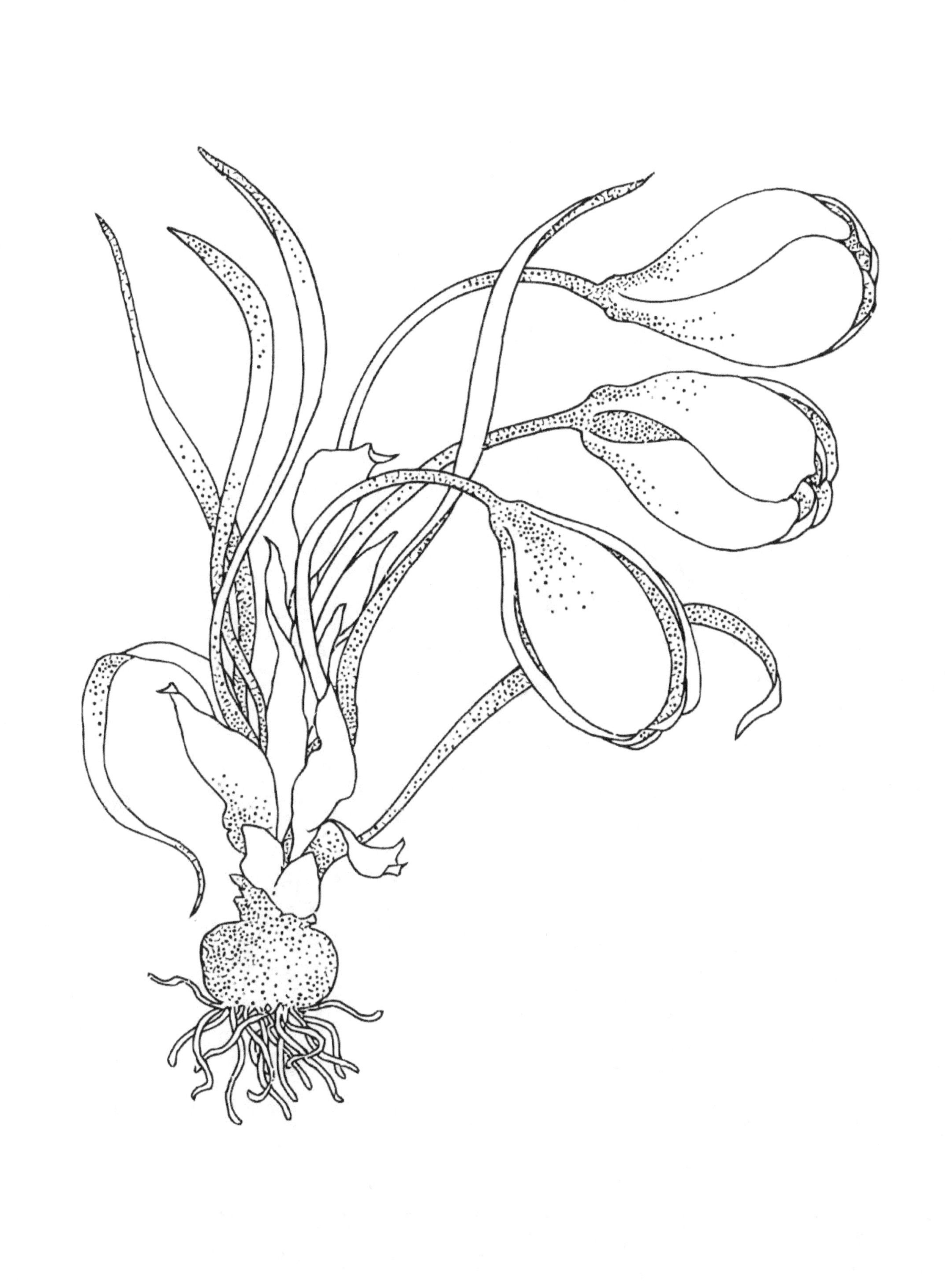

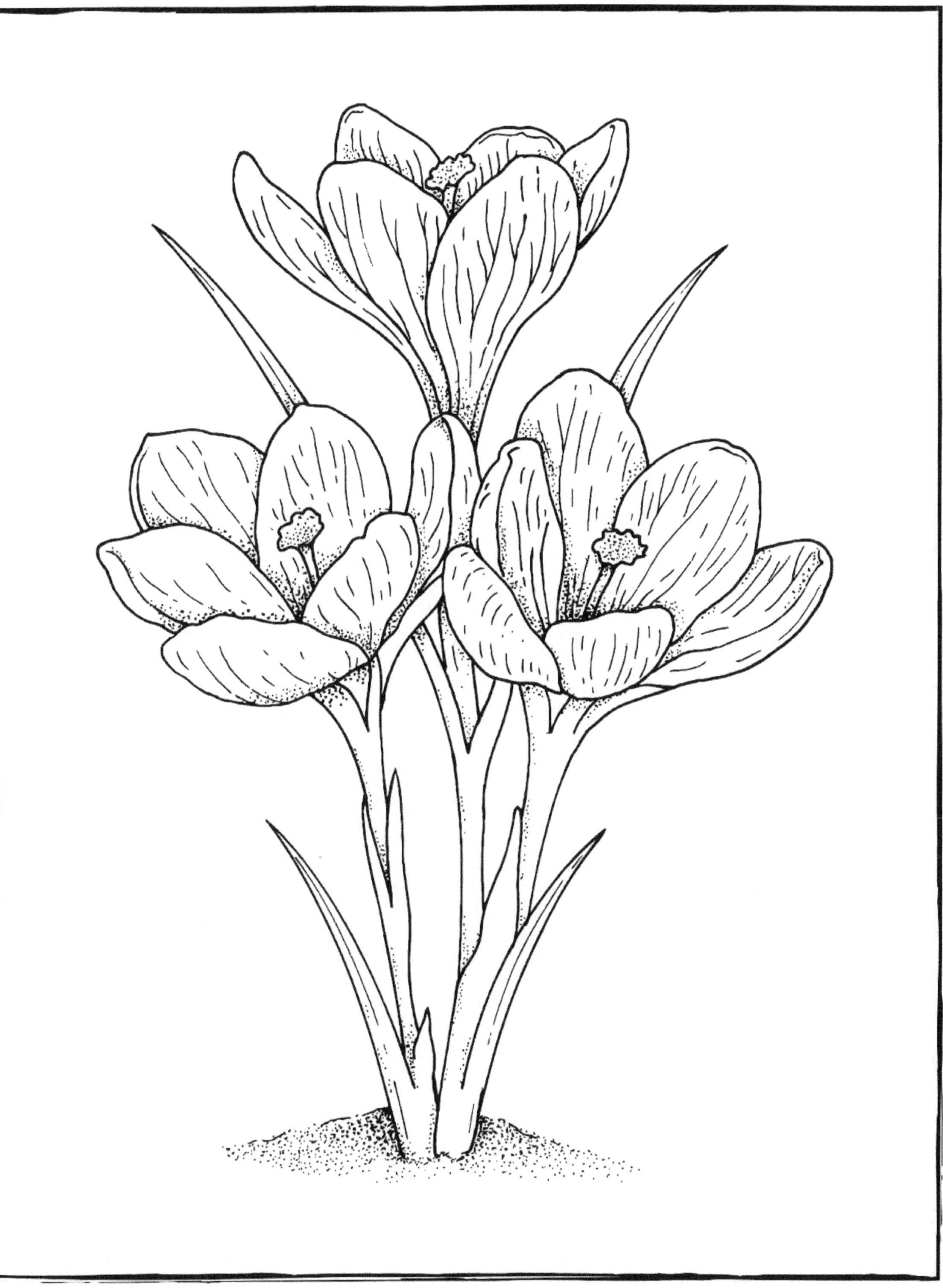

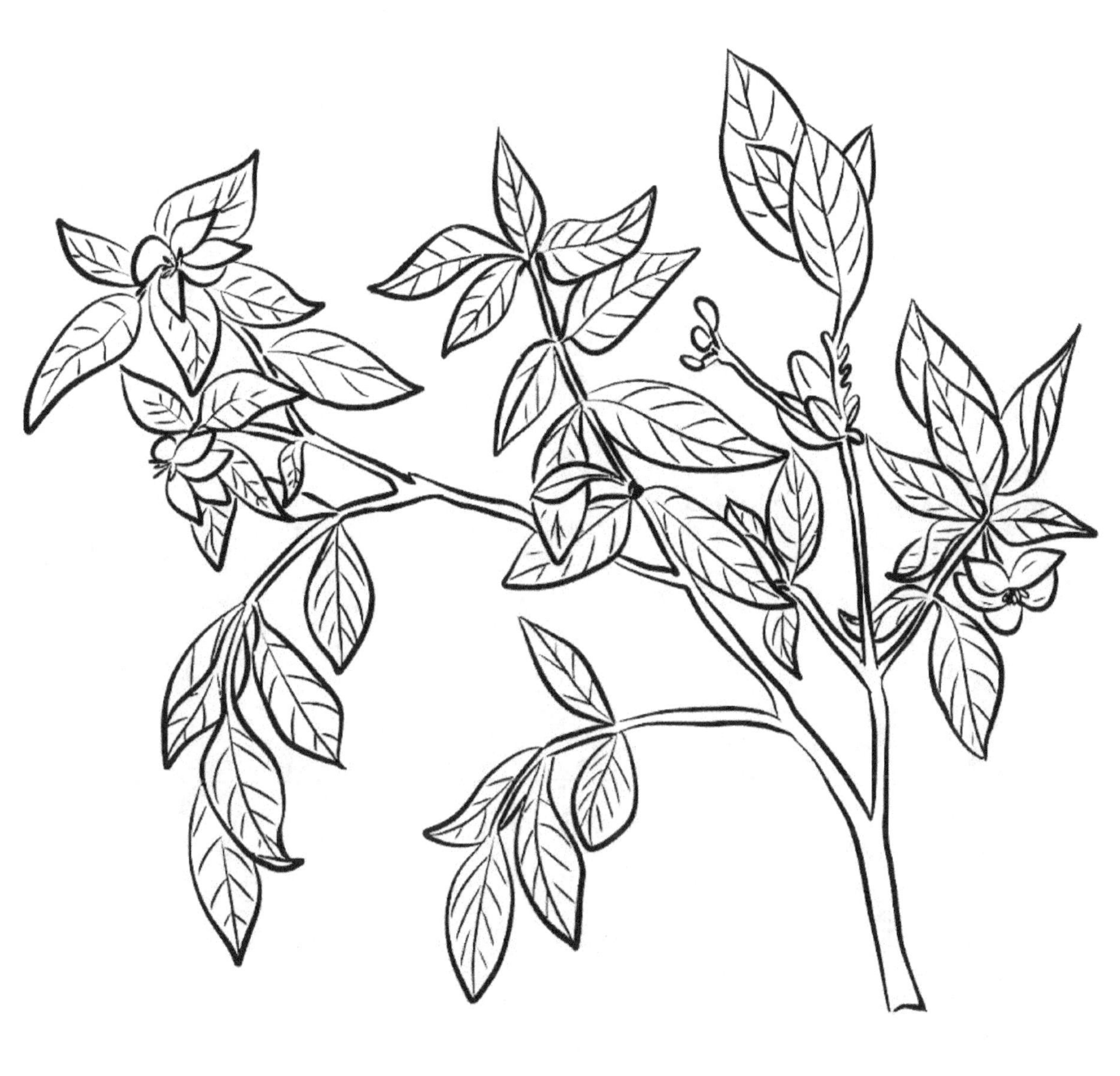

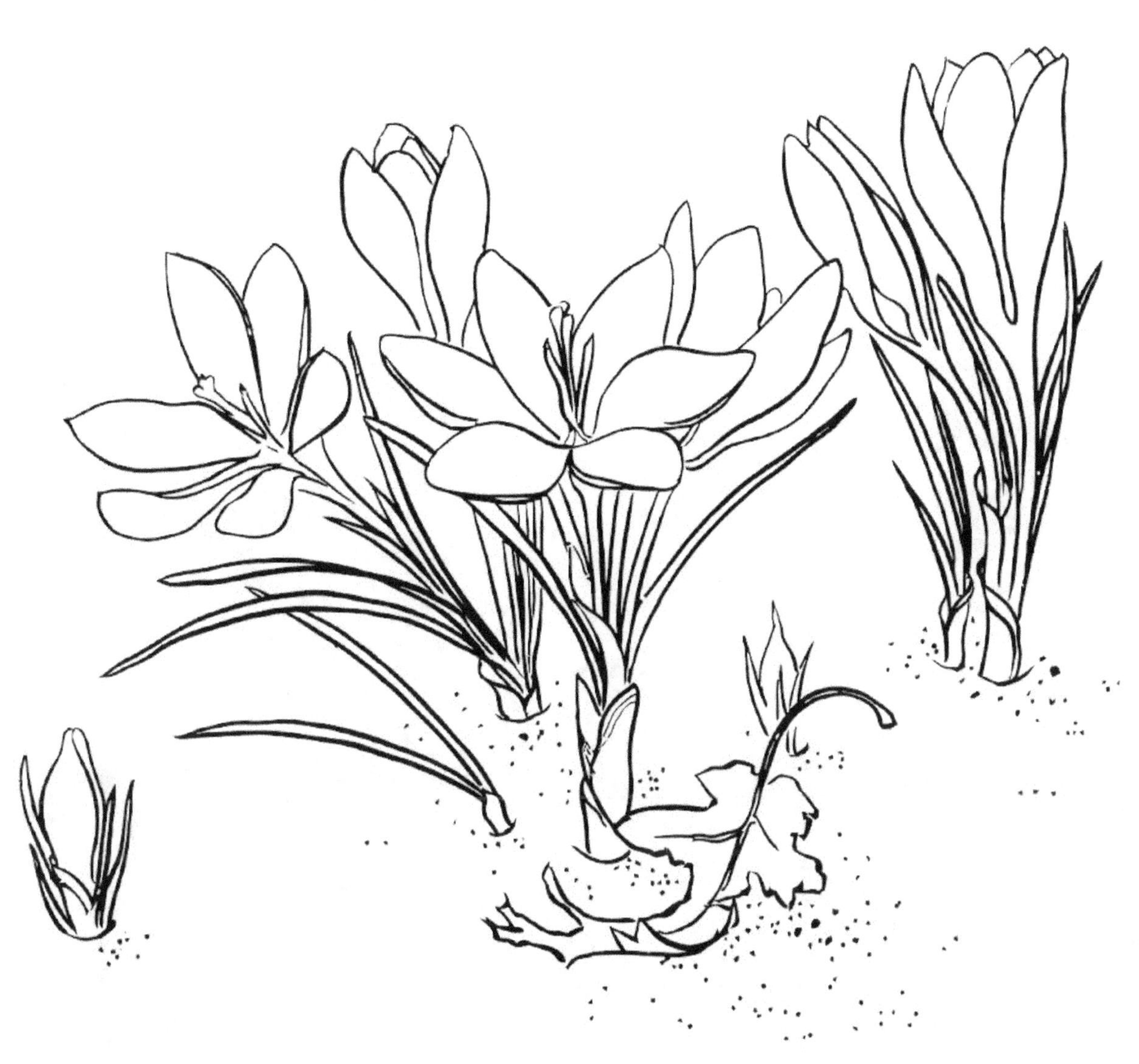

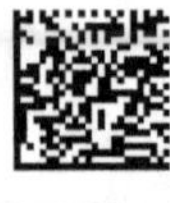

www.ingramcontent.com/pod-product-compliance
Lightning Source LLC
Chambersburg PA
CBHW081449250726
48662CB00009B/3007